★

How to Be a Texan

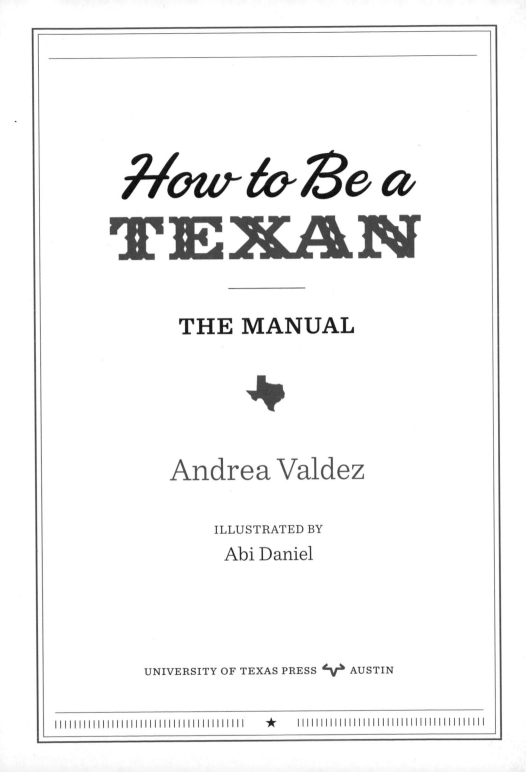

How to Be a TEXAN

THE MANUAL

Andrea Valdez

ILLUSTRATED BY

Abi Daniel

UNIVERSITY OF TEXAS PRESS ⛥ AUSTIN

This book is not intended to be a definitive resource for there is no substitute for learning certain skills firsthand from an experienced Texan.

Requests for permission to reproduce material from this work should be sent to:
    Permissions
    University of Texas Press
    P.O. Box 7819
    Austin, TX 78713-7819
    http://utpress.utexas.edu/index.php/rights-permissions

♾ The paper used in this book meets the minimum requirements of ANSI/NISO Z39.48-1992 (R1997) (Permanence of Paper).

Many of the essays included in *How to Be a Texan* were published previously in slightly altered form in *Texas Monthly*.

Library of Congress Cataloging-in-Publication Data

Valdez, Andrea, author.
How to be a Texan : the manual / Andrea Valdez ; illustrated by Abi Daniel. — First edition.
    pages   cm
  Includes bibliographical references.
  ISBN 978-1-4773-0931-5 (cloth : alk. paper)
  ISBN 978-1-4773-0932-2 (library e-book)
  ISBN 978-1-4773-0933-9 (non-library e-book)
1. Texas—Social life and customs—Miscellanea. 2. Texas—Description and travel—Miscellanea. 3. Texas—Social life and customs—Humor. 4. Texas—Description and travel—Humor. I. Daniel, Abi, illustrator. II. Title.
  F391.2.V35   2016
  976.4—dc23   2015035016

doi:10.7560/309315

★

*To Beau, the most
authentic Texan I know.*

Contents

★

How to Be a Texan

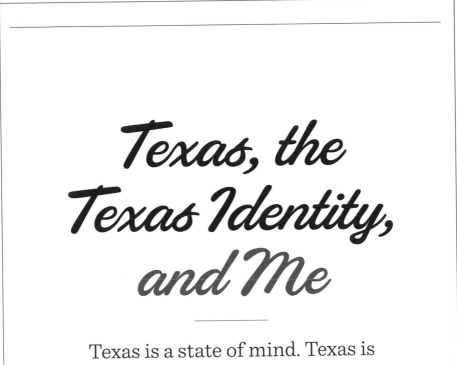

Texas, the Texas Identity, and Me

Texas is a state of mind. Texas is an obsession. Above all, Texas is a nation in every sense of the word.

John Steinbeck, *Travels With Charley: In Search of America*

Once when I was a kid, my mother made an offhand comment that forever shaped my perspective of my home state. I don't remember how it came up, though I assume it was during one of my obnoxious inquiries into her and my father's travels around the world to places far from our Houston home, like the tulip nurseries of the Netherlands, the Swatch stores in Switzerland, or the clean, cobbled streets of Germany. All I really recall is her telling me, "When people asked me where I was from, I never said America—I always said Texas."

I loved this detail. So much so that I vowed if I ever went abroad, I'd do the same. Invoking Texas—a place so universally recognized nearly everyone on the globe can point it out on a map—seemed to me to be a special privilege. At the very least, it could be an interesting conversation starter with exotic strangers.

When I embarked on my first big international trip, a ten-day excursion to Australia (a fitting destination as I always imagined it to be the Texas of the Southern Hemisphere), I figured this quirky fantasy would finally play out. As with most long-imagined daydreams, it didn't happen quite the way I thought it would. About halfway through the trip, my husband ordered a drink in a hotel lobby in Sydney. A man approached us and, with a broad smile on his face, declared, "I know *exactly* where you're from." In this case, it seemed we didn't have to identify as Texan; my husband's distinct (and charming) twang identified us.

Of course I'm proud to be American. I'm just also very proud to be Texan. I recognize this may seem silly—arrogant, even—but as any native Texan can attest to, we come by this inflated sense of self honestly . . . in part because the indoctrination starts so early. Like every kid in the United States, at the beginning of every school day I pledged allegiance to the United States of America. And, like every kid in Texas, I then pledged allegiance to the Lone Star State ("Honor the Texas Flag; I pledge allegiance to thee, Texas, one and indivisible"). By mandate of the state's board of education, the seventh-grade curriculum includes a Texas history class, where children learn about how Spanish explorers discovered our lands and how Sam Houston fought for those same lands. Even when I was in college at the University of Texas at Austin, students were allowed to take three credits of Texas history as a substitute for the American History requirement.

This Texas pride extended far beyond the classroom. There was almost no sight more ubiquitous to me than our state flag, and I long believed the myth that it was the only state banner that could legally fly as high as the American flag (a commonly repeated falsehood that sounds like it certainly could be true, given that Texas was once a sovereign nation). When companies mold products into the shape of Texas—from pies and waffle makers to a 168,000-gallon pool in Plano—it seems to me less like a marketing gimmick and more like a really good idea.

This almost blind affection for Texas became that much more apparent when I moved away to Chicago for graduate school. I lived in the Windy City for a year, and while the Midwest was friendly and I saw distinct seasons for the first time, I longed for home. I missed the shimmer of the Capitol Building's pink granite on a sunny day; the April bloom of spring bluebonnets and Indian paintbrushes dotting the highway in Washington County; the land so long and flat in northwest Texas that when the sun sets, it looks like it's on a slow collision course with the earth. Perhaps most deeply, I missed my personal soul food: Tex-Mex.

I thought the homesickness was natural, a knee-jerk reaction to leaving something familiar for something different. So I did what anyone with a strange obsession does: hurtle myself full force into it. I thickened my accent (none of the Midwesterners I spoke to knew what to make of the phrase "fixin' ta"). At potlucks, I made enchiladas, chiles rellenos, and fried chicken. I bought cowboy boots (that I never wore) and a stitched-leather belt. But most formatively, I became enamored of *Texas Monthly*, "the National Magazine of Texas." My parents had subscribed to the magazine off and on for years, and when I moved away, they mailed me old issues in care packages (along with my favorite tortilla chips and Wolf Brand Chili).

When I got a job at the publication just out of journalism school, it was my greatest dream realized. And during my decade-long tenure at the magazine, first as a fact-checker, then as the author of "The Manual," the column that shaped this book, and now as the editor of *Texas Monthly*'s website, my love for Texas has certainly intensified.

But it's also become significantly more nuanced.

Before, I was a bit of a Pollyanna about what it means to be Texan, buying into and repeating the myths. As I learn more about the state—and I do every day—I recognize it's a complicated place with a complicated history. When Álvar Núñez Cabeza de Vaca washed up on what is now known as Follet's Island, near present-day Galveston Island in the sixteenth century, he represented the start of a wave of conquistadors intent on exploiting new lands for gold, riches, and resources. The Alamo, which we are to never forget, has been the subject of innumerable books and papers extolling the "victory or death" attitude of the men inside the besieged church, but less ink has been spilled on explaining why the Mexicans were attacking them. When Abraham Lincoln issued the Emancipation Proclamation, abolishing slavery effective January 1, 1863, word didn't reach Texas until June 19, 1865, more than two years later, a travesty that meant enslaved men and women in our state lived an awful life that much longer.

Our recent history is also fraught. The assassination of John F. Kennedy, one of the greatest tragedies our nation has ever known, happened in 1963 in Dallas, earning Big D the unfortunate moniker "City of Hate," a disgraceful nickname it's been unable to shake, even decades later. Before Enron went bankrupt in 2001, becoming a textbook example of corporate greed run amok, it was one of the most visible business presences in Houston, a city that basked in the money while it lasted and turned on the company when it fell from grace. Even a place as culturally porous as our 1,200-mile border with Mexico remains one of the most controversial sites in the United States, sparking eternal debates over how to protect our international boundaries and manage immigration.

I understand that the rest of America—and the world—regards us warily, their negative preconceived notions born out of the stereotypes and misconceptions perpetuated by popular culture. But while our rancher roots, unassailable swagger, and maverick mentality might give someone the impression that we're a bunch of uneducated rubes or stubborn mules steadfast in our ways, Texas is always shifting, morphing, and evolving. We're not resistant to change; rather, we encourage discourse and argument, all in the name of sharpening and improving ideas. It's no accident that NASA chose

Houston as the home base for its Manned Spacecraft Center, that our doctors performed the first heart transplant in the US, that one of our oilmen is the father of fracking, and that Texas has produced countless other inventions and innovations. It's just that in our path to modernization, we've never been willing to forget our past. Texas is a pioneer state, and what is a pioneer but a person who paves a new trail with the bricks of tradition.

At times, when I've imagined living elsewhere, I remind myself of what the true Texas identity is—or actually, of what it has become—and I'm confident that it continues to represent the philosophies and values I hold important. I still want to tell the world I'm from this place, for this detail to be a conversation starter with exotic strangers.

This book is one more step on my quixotic quest to illuminate others about what it means to be Texan. In it, I lean into the enduring myths. And I deliberately curate what some might consider a Texas experience that kowtows to the clichés of our state. Sure, most people who own this book won't likely ever have the chance (or the *cojones*) to ride a bull, or the materials to tan a hide, or the patience to bake kolaches. But that doesn't mean that in a definitive guide to being Texan, you shouldn't be given the tools and advice to hop on and ride or roll up your sleeves if you're so inclined.

Some Texans who pick up this book might question or laugh at the topics I've chosen to include. Go ahead. Because just as there's more than one way to skin a deer, there's more than one way to be Texan. And I partake in and relish many of our newer traditions: I've stood in line at Franklin Barbecue in Austin and eaten

Vietnamese crawfish in Houston. I've zipped down I-10 going eighty-five miles per hour. I've trekked across state borders to gamble in Oklahoma and Louisiana. I've paid entirely too much for expensive leather goods simply because they were crafted in-state. But this isn't meant to be a reflection of the modern "Texas experience" (and now for my next book . . .); rather, this book is evidence that this place I love is the sum of *all* of those parts. Our culture has evolved in many ways, but Texas—maybe more than any other state—actively lives in its history. And it is that history that I want to be a part of for years to come.

Talk Like a
TEXAN

Texans don't just say the words;
they linger over them like they're old
friends, worthy of a cup of coffee.
It's the journey, not the destination,
that's important in a conversation.

Robert Hinkle, dialect coach for James Dean
and Rock Hudson, on the set of *Giant*

Americans have long celebrated—and imitated, and sometimes mocked—the charm of regional dialects. New Yorkers stretch single vowels into diphthongs ("dog" turns into "dooaugh"). Bostonians tend to drop *r*'s ("park the car at Harvard Yard" comes out as "pahk tha cah at Hahvahd yahd"). And Southerners, with their syrupy-sweet accent glazed with gentility, can deliver even the harshest insults in a way that sounds polite.

Yet over time there has been a steady erosion of regional accents. Linguists blame migration, urbanization, and, to some degree, the ascent of accent-neutral media for the homogenization of American English. And it appears Texas English is not immune to this phenomenon. In 2012 a number of news outlets sounded the alarm, reporting that the "Texas twang is dying." That year, Lars Hinrichs, the director of the University of Texas's Texas English Project, submitted a research paper that confirmed there was "dialect leveling" in urban areas. He later told the university's college paper, *The Daily Texan:* "The regional accents are no longer as pronounced and different as they used to be. . . . The degree of distinctiveness is being lessened and the linguistic local identity is being diluted. There will always be some local form of speech in Texas and it will always be noticeably different from other parts of the country—but not as much."

The state's distinct dialect may be shifting or declining, but the art of talking Texan endures. In fact, researchers have found that young Texans still embrace certain pronunciations, phrases, and accents, almost as a point of pride about their Texas identity. And for the native-born—especially those hailing from the rural areas—the deeply ingrained inflections indigenous to certain regions within the state are inherited passively, almost like a physical characteristic passed along from one generation to the next. There are the unmistakable nasally twang of West Texas, the soft drawl of the Piney Woods, and the Spanish-influenced dialect of the Rio Grande Valley, to name a few.

So even if you weren't born here, you can *git* along easy enough. Just remember that Texans operate from their own vocabulary, their own grammatical rules, and a learned style of pronunciation. And while some of the following phrases and sayings aren't unique to Texas, they're all part of the colorful way that we talk the talk.

★ ★ ★

ESSENTIAL VOCABULARY: WORDS AND PHRASES (AND ONE HAND GESTURE) YOU OUGHTA KNOW

blue norther: A term specific to Texas to describe a cold front that blasts in from the north. A blue norther is typically accompanied by precipitation and dark blue skies.

bumper crop: An exceptionally good crop harvest.

cattywampus: Out of line, or not quite right.

Coke: If you ask for a Coke at a restaurant, don't be surprised if someone asks, "What kind?" Every brown carbonated beverage—even a Dr Pepper—is referred to as a Coke.

Dr Pepper: This soda is native to Texas (Waco, specifically) and is often the preferred Coke option (see above) of most Texans. If you're writing out the brand's name, never put a period between Dr and Pepper.

drought vs. drouth: These days, most people say *drought* (rhymes with *snout*) when referring to a dry spell. *Drouth* (rhymes with *mouth*) is used by old-timers, West Texans, or people who survived the seven-year dry spell of the 1950s.

farm-to-market roads: These are state highways that were built for the purpose of bringing goods from the farms to, well, the market. The highway signage for farm-to-market roads, usually abbreviated FM, is a black square with a white shape of Texas bearing the number of the road. (Fun fact: There are also ranch-to-market roads, because ranchers couldn't stand the idea of their land being referred to as a farm.)

feeder road: The uninitiated in Houston might listen to a radio traffic report and think that the feeder road is both the longest road in all of the city and the one with the most congestion and accidents. However, *feeder road* is how Houstonians refer to freeway access roads.

fixin' ta': Few Texanisms inspire as much head cocking as the often-used and much-beloved phrase *fixin' ta'*. When someone informs you that he's "fixin' ta' [INSERT ACTION HERE]," he means he's getting ready to do something.

gully washer: A really heavy, really short storm.

hi sign: A one-finger wave (the index, not that one in

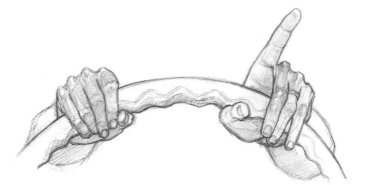

the middle) made when drivers pass each other on country roads. This gesture, which is generally made without ever lifting the hand from the wheel, is a courtesy of the road.

howdy: This friendly way of saying "hello" is admittedly on the wane, but as long as Big Tex, the fifty-five-foot-tall animatronic greeter for the State Fair of Texas, continues belting out his signature line, "Howdy, folks!," and it remains the official greeting at Texas A&M University, *howdy* will be a mainstay of Texas culture.

I reckon: The way a person starts—or ends—a sentence when he thinks something might be true but feels compelled to hedge his bets. Often used when referring to the weather, for example, "I reckon we'll see a blue norther blow through." Alternatively: "A blue norther's gonna blow through, I reckon."

might could: Used when someone could possibly do something (e.g., "I might could ride that mustang").

over yonder, or down yonder: Over there.

poleaxed: When someone is knocked down real hard, literally or figuratively.

supper vs. dinner: A term used interchangeably to refer to the evening meal, though some Texans refer to the midday meal as *dinner*. Language historians also report that *supper* referred to a simple meal at home while *dinner* was a more formal affair or an outing.

tank: A small, man-made pond, used primarily by livestock for drinking water.

tump over: To knock something over.

used to could: This highly ungrammatical phrase is a way to say you used to be able to do something (e.g., "I used to could two-step, but I haven't been dancing in years").

y'all: This second-person pronoun—a contraction of *you* and *all*—is used when talking to two or more people. *Y'all* also shows up as frequently in written form (especially on folksy magnets, stitched pillow cases, bumper stickers, and other knick-knacks found at any gas station in Texas), so when writing it out, be very mindful to place the apostrophe in the right place. Misplacing the apostrophe can land you in just as much grammatical hot water as putting a period after *Dr* in *Dr Pepper* (see above). Just like any other pronoun, it can be possessive ("How's y'all's day goin'?") and form contractions (*y'all* + *are* = *y'all're*). Sprinkle this word liberally throughout all y'all's conversations.

★ ★ ★

¿HABLAS SPANGLISH?

Given language's absorbent tendencies, the typical English speaker already knows a fair amount of Spanish. A number of Spanish words are so ingrained in our vocabularies, it's easy to forget they originated from another language (salsa, fiesta, rodeo). Others have been so fully incorporated into English that some people wouldn't even know they're Spanish—*arroyo* means stream; *armadillo*'s literal translation is "little armored one"; and *mosquito* is Spanish for "little fly." Nahuatl, the Aztec language, impressed itself upon Spanish too, giving us words like *avocado* (an Anglicization of *ahua-catl*), *coyote* (derived from the word *coyotl*), and *chile* (an adaptation of *chilli*).

In Texas, Mexican and American cultures have so thoroughly blended that it is common to toggle between English and Spanish, a practice known as code-switching. This commingling of vocabularies has led to a third, hybrid language known as *Spanglish*, an ever-evolving form of communication that bridges two communities. Below are a few key words and phrases to know.

Ándale pues: A phrase that indicates agreement, as in "That's totally right!"

borracho: "Drunk." (Related: *crudo*, Spanish for "hangover.")

carro: Slang for "car" (*coche* or *auto* are more proper terms).

chanclas: Slang for "house slippers" or "flip-flops."

¿Cómo está? or ¿Qué tal?: A formal way to say "How are you" or an informal greeting that means "What's up?"

Está bien: "It's okay" or "Everything is all right."

güero: A fair-skinned or light-haired person.

Hola: "Hello."

lonche: Spanglish for lunch (*almuerzo* is the correct Spanish word).

mi hijo/a or mi hijito/a): A term of endearment that

literally means "my son/daughter" (use the "o" for male pronouns and the "a" for female pronouns). Adding "ito" at the end means "my little son/daughter." Often pronounced as a conjunction, i.e. "Mi'jo/a."

órale: An exclamation that has many meanings, including "heck yes" or "okay!" Some people also use it as an exhortation, a way to say "come on!" or "hurry up."

parquear: Slang for park the car (estacionar is the correct word).

pachuco: A reference to young Mexican-Americans or Chicanos from the '30s and '40s who wore zoot suits and were considered rebellious. The term is said to have originated in El Paso.

panzón: A reference to a big belly, but often used as a good-natured nickname for friends with larger frames.

¡Qué gacho!: "How awful!" or "Not cool."

scuchale: A slang term that means "move over" or "scooch over."

troca: Spanglish for truck (the proper word is *camión*).

★ ★ ★

A HIGHLY IDIOSYNCRATIC SELECTION OF FAVORITE TEXAS SAYINGS

This ain't my first rodeo. Said if you are old hat or well versed in something.

She's all hat and no cattle. Used to describe someone

who talks a big game, but has no action to back up the bluster.

He's like a blister; he doesn't show up till the work's all done. Used to describe someone who is lazy.

It's the blueberry in the cherry pie. A humorous description of Austin and its liberal reputation when contrasted with the rest of Texas, which is considered a conservative, or red, state.

That dog'll hunt. Said when something will work or will do the trick.

I don't cotton to that. Said when someone doesn't like something or when something doesn't agree with a person.

It's drier than a popcorn fart. Used to describe hot and dry weather.

He's as dumb as a box of rocks. Used to describe someone who is not too bright.

If dumb were dirt, you'd be about an acre. A way to tell someone he's really dumb.

Everything but the moo. Said to describe how a butcher or hunter has used all the parts of a slaughtered animal.

She just fell off the turnip truck. Used to describe someone who is naïve or ignorant.

She was fit to be tied. Said when someone is extremely angry or upset.

It's good enough for government work. Describes a barely sufficient quality of work.

We're in high cotton. To be successful.

Don't have a hissy fit! When someone has a hissy fit, they are throwing a temper tantrum.

Nobody ever drowned in sweat. A proclamation to someone that they can work harder.

We looked like we'd been rode hard and put up wet. Originally referring to horses being stabled after exercise without being properly groomed, this is used to describe someone looking tired and haggard.

Smells like money. A positive spin on the literal smell of the oil fields of West Texas, which some consider offensive or unpleasant.

I was sweatin' like a whore in church. Used to describe someone who is very nervous.

He's so tight, he squeaks. Describes someone who is stingy.

Well, I'll be dipped. An exclamation used to describe surprise.

Who stuck the burr under your saddle?: "Why are you so agitated?"

You can't beat that with a stick. Said when referring to a good deal.

You can take that to the bank. Said as a guarantee on the quality of something.

★ ★ ★

YOU'RE SAYING IT WRONG: A PRONUNCIATION GUIDE TO PLACES IN TEXAS

Bexar: BAY-er, or rhymes with *bear*.

Boerne: BURN-ee.

Bowie: BOO-ee (Not BOW-ee, like the rock star).

Buda: BYOO-duh.

Burnet: BURN-it. (Or, as locals like to say, "Burnet, dernit. Learn it!")

Eldorado: El-doe-RAY-doe.

Elgin: EL-gen, with a hard *g*.

Falfurrias: Fal-FOO-rhee-us.

Gruene: GREEN, just like the color.

Guadalupe: Gwad-ah-LOOP-eh.

Iraan: Ira-ANN.

Llano: LAN-o, though when referring to the Llano Estacado, use the Spanish pronunciation of "yahn-o."

Manchaca: MAN-chack. For no known reason, the final *a* is silent.

Manor: MAY-ner, not lord of the manor.

Marathon: MARA-thun.

Mexia: Muh-HAY-uh.

Miami: My-AM-uh.

Nacogdoches: Nack-uh-DOE-chess.

New Braunfels: Often said with an *s* after *Braun*, an inaccurate pronunciation.

Pedernales: Per-den-AL-es.

Quitaque: Kit-uh-KEW.

Refugio: Despite not having an *r after the* f sound, it's pronounced Re-FUR-ee-o.

San Antonio: Calling the city "San Antone" is a surefire way to let people know you aren't from Texas.

San Jacinto: In Spanish, the *j* has an *h* sound (San Huh-sint-o), but most Texans pronounce this with a true *j* sound (San Juh-cent-o). Some even shorten it to San Jack.

Waxahachie: As much as you want to say "wax" to start off this word, it's wahks-uh-HATCH-ee.

★ ★ ★

ROOT FOR THE HOME TEAM

Texas A&M University and the Aggies
The students and alumni of Texas A&M University have their own language. As they often say, "It's an Aggies thing. You wouldn't understand." Below, a few of the more common terms you might hear from the mouths of Aggies. (It should be noted this list is far from comprehensive, and more resources can be found under Further Reading.)

12th Man: A tradition born on January 2, 1922, the 12th Man is the whole student body, which stands during the entire game in the event that the eleven players on the gridiron need assistance.

BTHO: An acronym for "beat the hell outta" the opposing team.

Corps of Cadets: The oldest student organization on campus, these students head into all of the branches of the military.

Gig 'em: This thumbs-up gesture was the first hand sign of the Southwest Conference. The origin of the tradition is attributed to "Pinky" Downs, a member of A&M's Board of Regents, who was amping up the crowd at a Yell Practice (see below) before a game against Texas Christian University in 1930. He asked what the Aggies would do to TCU's Horned Frogs and replied to himself, saying, "gig 'em!" a reference to gigging, a practice used to hunt frogs.

Midnight Yell Practice: A glorified pep rally held the night before football games to amp up the fans.

Tea-sip (or t-sip) and t.u.: Derogatory or dismissive terms used by the Aggies for students and alumni of the University of Texas as well as the University itself ("t.u." stands for "Texas university," to emphasize that UT is one of *many* Texas universities, rather than the only one).

Whoop: An exclamatory cry of joy or approval. Only juniors and seniors can use this word.

Yell Leaders: The five male upperclassmen who are

voted into their positions as the "Keepers of the Spirit" of Aggieland. They lead Midnight Yell practice.

The University of Texas and the Longhorns
While UT fans are equally passionate about their school as A&M, their lexicon is not nearly as elaborate or as involved as the school's former in-state rival. But if you step on the Forty Acres (a.k.a. campus), here are a few things you should know.

Bevo: The name of UT's mascot, a longhorn steer that is cared for by a student organization called the Silver Spurs.

Big Bertha: Proclaimed by the school to be the "world's largest bass drum," Big Bertha, the "sweetheart of the Longhorn Band," is eight feet in diameter and 41 inches wide.

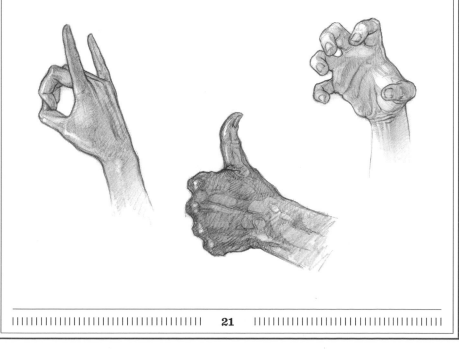

"The Eyes of Texas": One of the University of Texas's school spirit songs, sung to the tune of "I've Been Working on the Railroad." Learn the lyrics. Love them. Live them.

> *The Eyes of Texas are upon you,*
> *All the livelong day.*
> *The Eyes of Texas are upon you,*
> *You cannot get away.*
> *Do not think you can escape them*
> *At night or early in the morn—*
> *The Eyes of Texas are upon you*
> *'Til Gabriel blows his horn.*

Hook 'Em: The Longhorns' hand signal, in which the two middle fingers curve down and are held by the thumb as the index and pinky fingers create a horn shape.

Texas Fight: The official school fight song, which is often sung directly after the "Eyes of Texas" and following touchdowns and extra points.

> *Texas Fight, Texas Fight,*
> *And it's goodbye to A&M.*
> *Texas Fight, Texas Fight,*
> *And we'll put over one more win.*
> *Texas Fight, Texas Fight,*
> *For it's Texas that we love best.*
> *Hail, Hail, The gang's all here,*
> *And it's good-bye to all the rest! (YELL)*
> *Yea Orange! Yea White!*
> *Yea Longhorns! Fight! Fight! Fight!*

Texas Fight! Texas Fight,
Yea Texas Fight!
Texas Fight! Texas Fight,
Yea Texas Fight!

A few other schools have notable traditions including...

Baylor University

Dr Pepper Hour: For decades, the famously conservative Baylor congregation have engaged in this wonderfully saccharine social hour, where Dr Pepper floats are served to the student body.

Sic 'em, Bears: The rally cry for fans. For the full effect, paw your hand in the air like you're mauling the opponent.

Kilgore College

The Rangerettes: This world-famous dance troupe was founded in 1939 by Gussie Nell Davis. Their synchronized choreography mesmerizes audiences, prompting the Houston Contemporary Museum of Art to go so far as to declare the style of dance a "living form of art."

Rice University

The MOB: This Ivy League-caliber university's football team may have a high IQ, but the Owls have spent many years in the dregs of their conference. (Granted, like many programs, they have highs and lows, albeit a few more of the latter than the former.) However, the Marching Owl Band—a misnomer as the band declares that they "don't march. Ever."—is one of the highlights of football games for the Houston-based school. During halftime, they often rush the field as a crazy swarm of instruments and legs before locking into place and performing some of the most hilarious and irreverent band formations in college football history.

Texas Tech

Guns Up: The hand signal of the Red Raiders, a finger-gun pointing up in the air.

High School Bonus

"Clear Eyes, Full Hearts, Can't Lose": This line from the television show *Friday Night Lights*—a program inspired by the book *Friday Night Lights*, which is based on the real-life 1988 Permian Panthers high school football team—may be spoken by a fictional coach, Coach Eric Taylor, to a fictional team, but these inspirational words have permeated the state's popular culture, becoming a battle cry appropriate for nearly all situations.

★ ★ ★

DON'T MESS WITH TEXAS: MORE THAN A SLOGAN

Everyone knows the phrase, but before it was part of the national consciousness, "Don't mess with Texas" was simply meant to be an anti-littering marketing campaign. Created by the ad wizards at GSD&M (a Texas-based company) for the Department of Highways and Public Transportation—now the Texas Department of

Transportation—the slogan debuted on television in January 1986 in a thirty-second spot that aired during the fiftieth annual Cotton Bowl. In it, Stevie Ray Vaughan, the legendary blues guitarist from Dallas, plays "The Eyes of Texas" as a voiceover says, "Each year we spend over $20 million picking up trash along our Texas highways. Messing with Texas isn't just an insult to the Lone Star State; it's a crime." Vaughan looks up, declares, "Don't mess with Texas," and the phrase becomes forever a part of our identity.

★ ★ ★

FURTHER READING

Atwood, Elmer Bagby. *The Regional Vocabulary of Texas.* Austin: University of Texas Press, 1962.

Chariton, Wallace O. *This Dog'll Hunt: An Entertaining Texas Dictionary.* Plano, TX: Woodware Publishing, 1989.

Dingus, Anne. *More Texas Sayings Than You Can Shake a Stick At.* Houston: Gulf Publishing Company, 1996.

Heathman, Claire. "Aggie Glossary: On 'Gig 'em,' 'howdy,' 'hump it' and 'whoop'." MyAggieNation.com. http://www.myaggienation.com/history_traditions/aggie_glossary/.

2

Look Like a TEXAN

Here it is better to be a drugstore
cowboy than no cowboy at all.

Larry McMurtry, *In a Narrow Grave*

There are few stereotypes of Texas more crystal-
lized in the national consciousness than how
we dress: ten-gallon hats, boots clanging with
silver spurs, pressed Wranglers, pearl-snap
button-downs. The Texas myth is clothed in this cowboy
uniform and it's been perpetuated by some of our state's
most famous celebrities. Tioga native Gene Autry, the
"Singing Cowboy," popularized the gimmicky Western
getup back in the thirties and forties with his elabo-
rately embroidered shirts and knotted neck scarf. (His
flashy fashion had a strong assist from Nudie Cohn, one
of country music's most influential designers.) Uvalde
native Dale Evans, the wife of Roy Rogers, feminized the

Western look with her tasseled and fringed yoked shirts, rhinestone-studded belts, and embossed white boots. Together they symbolized an era of Western glamour that people still associate with drugstore cowboys.

Then there's George Strait, the "King of Country," whose aesthetic favors a more stripped-down, classic cowboy look. His embodiment of the wholesome good ol' boy made him the perfect spokesman for Wrangler jeans, Resistol hats, and Justin Boots, and for nearly thirty years, cardboard cutouts of his likeness wearing these brands have been displayed in Cavender's and Sheplers stores across Texas. It is also worth noting that Strait's star rose during the '80s, which was also the *Urban Cowboy* decade. That movie, set in a honky-tonk in Pasadena, Texas, launched what was quite possibly the biggest revival of country-inspired fashion. However Hollywood, being Hollywood, dudded up its protagonists Sissy and Bud in silver-studded boot tips, satin two-toned Western shirts, and belt buckles half as big as a man's face.

But not every country cowboy (or wannabe) has embraced being so shiny and polished. During the '70s, Waylon and Willie and the boys of the outlaw country movement wore a slightly grimier, hippified version of these country clothes: well-worn straw cowboy hats, cigarette-soot-encrusted jeans, and worn T-shirts. Throwing off the, ahem, yoke of the traditional Western shirt was a bit of a middle finger to the Nashville establishment. (And because everything old becomes new again, this look has come back into style; the wardrobe of fashionable hipsters in Austin is clearly influenced by the "cosmic cowboys" of the '70s.)

But it's not all boots, belts, and jeans in Texas. People

often forget that Neiman Marcus, a pillar of haute couture, opened in 1907 in Dallas, becoming one of the first stores to offer ready-to-wear fashion to women in Texas. In the '90s, Saks Fifth Avenue opened its second-largest store in Houston's Galleria, the upscale mall where Neiman Marcus sold more couture than any of its other stores in the nation. When Sakowitz was still a chain, French designers André Courrèges and Yves Saint Laurent debuted new or exclusive lines at the clothing store's Texas locations. In 2013 Karl Lagerfeld, the artistic director for Chanel, hosted an extravagant showcase of couture in Dallas, further cementing the city's legacy as a fashion hub.

And Texas has produced some of the nation's greatest fashion icons. Jerry Hall, the six-foot-tall blonde from Gonzales, graced the cover of dozens of magazines, including *Vogue* and *Cosmopolitan,* before capturing the attention of Mick Jagger, whom she later married. Suzy Parker, who was raised in San Antonio, was the muse for photographer Richard Avedon. The iconic image of Farrah Fawcett, the stunner from Corpus Christi, wearing a red swimsuit, feathered golden tresses, and a perfectly toothy smile hung on the bedroom walls of teenaged boys across America. And the Dallas Cowboy Cheerleaders—the squad praised as much for their athleticism as for their attractive members clad in their famous blue-and-silver Western-style uniforms— is a cultural institution known the world over.

Even specific fashion accessories have become inextricably linked to our heritage: Davy Crockett's coonskin cap, Selena's handmade bedazzled bustiers and bolero jackets, Tom Landry's hat, Lydia Mendoza's colorful rebozos, Buddy Holly's black horn-rimmed glasses, and Willie Nelson's braids.

And we don't just wear it; Texans have also built fashion empires. Dallasite Mary Kay Ash started a makeup company with $5,000 in 1963, and, despite the ubiquity of similar products in malls, drugstores, and everywhere in between, the direct retailer is now worth $3 billion. The famous pink Cadillac given to top saleswomen still captures the nation's imagination. Jessica Simpson, another blonde from Dallas, has a retail brand worth more than $1 billion (clearly she isn't nearly as ditzy as some think). Amber Venz, also from Dallas, figured out how to manipulate technology in such a way that she's made fashion bloggers—and herself—a few pretty pennies. And then, of course, there's Beyonce Knowles, the Houstonian who has become a global sensation, whose sartorial influence can set off an immediate trend.

The takeaway is this: no matter what you choose to wear, be it boots or bolo ties or Balenciaga, don it with Texas pride.

★ ★ ★

BUY CUSTOM COWBOY BOOTS

When the 80th Legislature named cowboy boots the state shoe in 2007, the resolution's authors described the footwear as "one of the most treasured of Texas icons," one that "play[s] a valued role in one of the defining chapters in Texas history and continue[s] to figure in the mythic romance of the Lone Star State." That's no small duty to lay at the feet of a pair of shoes.

This burden of responsibility extends to the wearer, and there are few sartorial decisions of more importance than choosing the right pair of boots. While you aren't supposed to judge a book by a cover, no one in Texas would fault you for judging a man by his footwear. And for good reason; your cowboy boots say a lot about you. Scuffed-up Tony Lamas betray long hours on the ranch; pristine glossy eelskin signals one's delicate nature; and personalized flair can tell another person—quite literally, if you opt for stitched initials or a last name— who you are.

To be honest, as rural populations shrink and urban cores boom, cowboy boots have become more of a fashion statement and less of a workwear item. But still, when in Texas, do as the Texans do and buy a pair. Because if the highly-customized shoe fits . . .

Leather

Your quest for inimitable footwear begins with the leather, so first give thought to your stomping grounds (cattle pen or cubicle?) and your image ("Rhinestone Cowboy"?). Your basic, most traditional option is calf-skin. Need extra-tough work boots? Elephant, shark, or bull offers durability. Dress boots? Go with lizard,

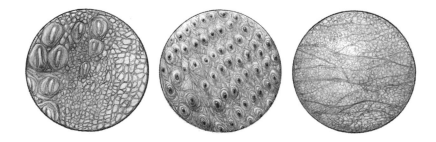

stingray, ostrich, or crocodile. And then there's kanga-roo. "The cashmere of leathers," says Nevena Christi, co-owner of Rocketbuster Boots, in El Paso, the Boot Capital of the World. "Soft, sturdy—and expensive."

Height

Determine the height of the top. Vintage-style cowgirl short-tops, known as "peewees," come in at ten or eleven inches—all the better to show off those sexy stems—while "buckaroos," which can measure up to twenty inches, protect a working cowboy from brush and bramble. Unless you actually own a horse, stick to the standard: twelve to fourteen inches.

Pulls

Jennifer June, the author of *Cowboy Boots: The Art and Sole*, will tell you that pulls come in four basic varieties: outside pulls (visible when you lift your cuff), inside pulls (which sit within the boot), mule ears (extra-long decorative loops), or just plain holes. Practical, yes, but also a place for flair: "Add color, a Texas flag, or your initials," she suggests.

Design

Stitching is the most common design feature. You can also request inlays and overlays, colorful cutouts beneath or on top of the boot's leather. And then there's tooling, a luxury option. Custom boots can cost $2,500 or more (turnaround time ranges from six weeks to a year). But if you're spending the money anyway, have fun: Request foxing (overlays on the toe or heel), a collar (decorative leather along the top of the boot), or brightly colored piping (narrow trim on the seams).

Heel

The average heel comes in at around one and a half inches. But conventions are for ignoring, especially by the fairer sex, who can pull off as much as two to three inches, or by some cowboys, who like the height for better stirrup grip. Most boots are made with underslung heels: "The sharper the angle, the more dramatic and stylish your look," says Scott Wayne Emmerich, co-founder of the Tres Outlaws boot company in El Paso. Roper-style heels are the low, walking kind, good if you're required to follow a corporate dress code.

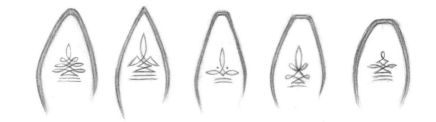

Toe

The toe says everything. Pointy is the province of fashionistas and Hollywood; real ranchers gravitate toward a round look. Hipsters rock the box toe. Boardroom types go for the slightly squared-off French style. (Your bootmaker, on the other hand, will refer to different toe shapes by letters such as *U*, *J*, or *X*.) Above all, consider your image. Mosey into your local honky-tonk with broad, round toes, and you say, "I just broke the new palomino." Opt for ultra-tapered ends, and you probably pronounce "rodeo" "ro-*day*-o."

★ ★ ★

ATTACH SPURS TO THOSE BOOTS

Any rodeo fan can don a Stetson, Wranglers, and a pair of Justins, but the cowboys in the arena are the ones who wear the spurs. "It's like a knight in his armor," says Joe Spiller, who's been handcrafting them for more than two decades and owns Spiller Spurs & Bits, in Wingate. The jangling accessories started out as a utilitarian training tool—riders use them to give movement cues to an animal by applying pressure to its sides—but they have also become a sort of social statement. "People wear them to personalize an outfit," Spiller says, and the design you choose should reflect their purpose. Working cowboys prefer simplicity, while ranch owners signal their clout with elaborate scrolling. But no matter who you are, be courteous and slip them off before entering someone's home.

The Fit

Each spur comes with spur straps. Button one end of the strap onto the hanger's hinge, a round piece of metal on either end of the heel band. With the hinges pointing up, place the spur on the spur ledge, which is the protruding edge of a boot heel. Pull the strap around the vamp, or front of the boot, and button the strap onto the opposite hinge. Tighten the buckle.

The Parts

A spur has three components: the heel band, the shank, and the rowel. As its name suggests, the heel band, a U-shaped piece of metal, wraps around the boot's heel.

Extending from the middle of the heel band is the shank. "The taller the person, the longer the shank needs to be to accommodate the position of his leg in relation to the animal," Spiller says. The rowel, a rotating disk with blunt points, is attached to the shank tip. A rowel with fewer points is more severe, because less surface area touches the animal.

The Flair

"Every aspect of a spur can be customized," Spiller says, including the metal, which can be carbon steel (traditional), iron (heavy), aluminum (light), or stainless steel (shiny). Customers ask him to engrave initials or intricate illustrations into heel bands, design "gal legs" (shanks that look like a lady's gams), or stylize the rowels by increasing their diameter and number of points. You can also shine the spurs to a high gloss or let a natural patina develop. "All I ask," says Spiller, whose custom creations range from $1,500 to $5,000, "is that you wash off the mud and poop."

★ ★ ★

CHOOSE A BELT BUCKLE

Western-yoke, pearl-snap plaid shirts and straight-fit jeans may go in and out of style, but custom-made belt buckles will always be classic. "It's an item you can wear every day for the rest of your life, then pass down to the

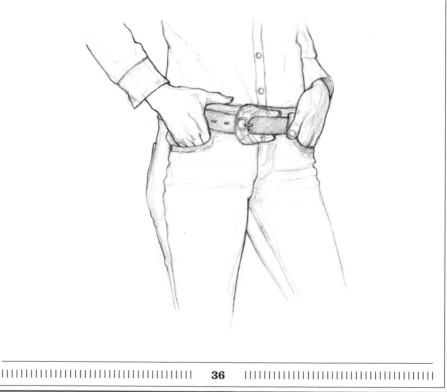

next generation," says Ingram's Clint Orms, who, during his three decades as a silversmith, has crafted buckles for clients ranging from ranch hands to Ralph Lauren. But the style befitting a cowgirl in Alpine might not be best for a bank president in Dallas. "The backbone of my design is the thought of the trophy buckle, but there are more understated options," Orms says. "You don't have to feel like you just stepped out of the trailer with Sissy."

The Type

While the trophy buckle is "part of the character of Texas," according to Orms, and may be the preference for cowboys (real or drugstore), ordinary folks who don't own a ranch should consider a horseshoe-style buckle. Typically, this comes in a three- or four-piece set that comprises a buckle, one or two "keepers" (the loops that hold the belt tongue), and a decorative tip.

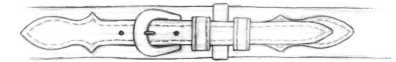

The Design

Before commissioning a piece from a silversmith, pick your metal: bronze, steel, sterling silver, or myriad shades of gold. Then consider your design (classic Texas star? silver longhorn with gold horns?) and your embellishments, which can include personalized engraving, intricate scrolling, or inset jewels. But if you want something elaborate, be patient. "A craftsman can spend up to two hundred hours on a buckle," says Orms. Perhaps

more important, be prepared to pay: time-consuming pieces made with precious metals and stones can cost tens of thousands of dollars.

The Style

If you opt for the horseshoe-style buckle, consider your wardrobe when choosing the width, which typically comes in one inch or three-fourths of an inch. The smaller size lends a dressier flair and looks better on thinner belts. And speaking of the actual belt, or strapping, this is another place to enhance style: choose a material (classic calfskin, dressy lizard), a hue (black for formal occasions or caramel for the ranch), and stitching or stamping for additional personalization (if you're into coordination, it can even match the design on your custom boots). Specify if you want a straight or tapered end, and the craftsman will be sure the decorative tip fits the belt's tongue. For an authentically Western look, ask for a Ranger belt, made famous by the Texas lawmen who used the additional leather strapping in front as holsters for their pistols.

The Style

Once all the components are selected, the craftsman will screw the custom buckle onto the leather (don't worry; this is easy to transfer when a belt wears out). Trophy buckles attach a little differently. The belt strap has a set of snaps on one end and belt holes on the other. Slip the end with the snaps through the loop on the back of the buckle, and snap closed. Slide the belt through your pant loops, then fit the prong through the hole on the opposite side.

Wearing the buckle is the best way to prevent tarnish, but Orms suggests you also give it a quick buff once a month with a polishing cloth. "It should get the same care that you'd use on a tea set."

★ ★ ★

WEAR A COWBOY HAT

A cowboy hat is a beloved possession: It fans fires, it blocks the rain, it gives shade—and it lends authenticity at any honky-tonk or rodeo. But it's also an extension of one's personality, so commissioning one takes serious thought (and serious dough: from $300 to $1,500). The first decision? Felt or straw. Felt hats are made from varying gradations of beaver and rabbit furs, 100 percent beaver being the best quality, while high-caliber straw hats are woven from Mexican palm leaves. The pros and cons: Felt is water-repellent, but it traps heat; straw

allows breezes to circulate, but it lets UV rays through. And while a straw hat may be cheaper, it shares the shelf life of a gallon of milk, whereas a felt hat may easily outlast your dairy cow.

The Style

"A well-made hat tells a story about the individual wearing it," says Chuck Wilkerson, the co-owner of Mike's Custom Hatters in Longview and the official outfitter for Missouri's Roy Rogers-Dale Evans Museum until it closed in 2009. Most shops offer a wide variety of brims (widths range from four to five inches) and crown styles, such as the flat-topped Gambler and the pear-shaped Tycoon creases or the subtle Montana pinch. At Mike's, ranch hands order the Cattleman, a classic wide-brimmed model with a prominent center crease and two deep crown tucks. Choose from just about any color, but if you plan on *actually* roping little dogies, pass on pure white—ivory resists dirty work much better.

The Fit

Take heed lest you measure improperly and fall victim to a common malady: hat headache. "Wrap the tape around your head about a half inch above the brow bone and the ear," says Kelly Owens, the co-owner of Limpia Creek Custom Hats in Fort Davis, a company given the sole honor of creating replicas of hats once worn by John Wayne. "Measure the circumference of your head to the nearest eighth of an inch, divide by pi (3.14), and that's your hat size." Also be prepared to answer a few fitting questions. Do hats leave red marks on your forehead? Your head is probably oval-shaped. Do they leave you tender above the ears? Your head is likely a uniform sphere.

The Flair

No cowboy headgear is complete without a hatband, that fashionable necessity used to cover up the hatter's stitchwork on the sweatband. The traditional choice? A simple felt strip matching the hat color, fastened with a small buckle. Braided leather lends a rustic look, while a gold chain with diamonds can send a message about your recent interest in the Eagle Ford Shale. The options, in short, are limitless: West Texans are said to favor turquoise-studded bands; South Texans go for silver conchos; and cowgirls statewide have been known to request tassels, good-luck trinkets, or feathers. (*Note:* Elaborate requests cost more money.) You might even channel your inner Duke and order an engraved sterling silver hatband. Talk about a *real* feather in your cap.

⋆ ⋆ ⋆

GET BIG HAIR

Texas women may not have invented big hair, but they realized long ago the allure of the coiffed crown. Just consider Ann Richards, who made it her trademark and declared an official Big Hair Day in 1993. The style is powerful yet elegant, bold but surprisingly down-home.

As Gail Huitt, the former governor's hairdresser, who has been a stylist in Austin for more than four decades, points out, "Nothing is worse than a big-butted woman with a little head."

Though the look never fell flat here, hair-up-to-there periodically sees style revival across the country. Jessica Simpson, the Texas-born-and-bred blonde bombshell, released a line of clip-on extensions in the 2000s; infomercials for the Bumpit, a leave-in volumizing insert, once dominated late-night airwaves; and Vera Wang once requested that her models wear modified beehives for a runway show. Thankfully, you don't need tons of hair to have big hair (Richards had baby-fine strands, Huitt says); all you need is a can—or three—of hairspray and a fine-toothed comb and you, too, can have the kind of 'do that inspired this incredible Texas-ism: "the taller the hair, the closer to God."

Wash

Some hairdressers swear by dirty hair—the scalp's oils are like a natural hair product—but Huitt recommends starting with freshly washed locks. Wick away moisture with a towel, and then apply a volumizing product at the roots.

Dry

Flip your hair upside down and blow-dry completely with a diffuser attachment, which creates even more volume. Using the pointed end of a rattail comb, part the hair about two inches back from either your hairline or bang line.

Tease

Back-comb the sectioned hair at the roots and spray each teased piece with a(n) (un)healthy dose of Aqua Net hairspray. Continue parting, teasing, and spraying your way back toward your crown. Gently smooth out the top with your comb.

Spray

Curl and pin the ends if desired. Set the hair into an impenetrable helmet by fogging down the 'do one last time. "After that, don't touch it," says Huitt. "As soon as you put your hands in your hair, you break the fragile bonds of the product—or a fingernail."

★ ★ ★

FURTHER READING

Beard, Tyler. *Art of the Boot*. Layton, UT: Gibbs Smith, 1999.

June, Jennifer. *Cowboy Boots: The Art & Sole*. New York: Universe, 2007.

Mills, Betty J. *Calico Chronicle: Texas Women and Their Fashions, 1830–1910*. Lubbock: Texas Tech University Press, 1985.

Walker, Myra. *Balenciaga and His Legacy: Haute Couture from the Texas Fashion Collection*. New Haven, CT: Yale University Press, 2006.

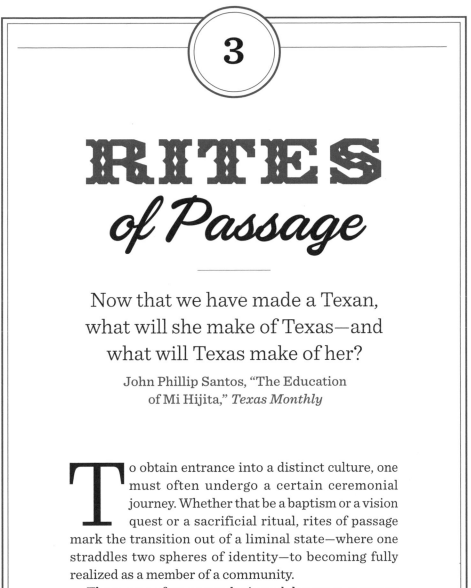

3

RITES
of Passage

Now that we have made a Texan,
what will she make of Texas—and
what will Texas make of her?

John Phillip Santos, "The Education
of Mi Hijita," *Texas Monthly*

T o obtain entrance into a distinct culture, one
must often undergo a certain ceremonial
journey. Whether that be a baptism or a vision
quest or a sacrificial ritual, rites of passage
mark the transition out of a liminal state—where one
straddles two spheres of identity—to becoming fully
realized as a member of a community.

These acts often occur during adolescence or young
adulthood, and this is no exception in Texas. Kids as
young as eight are given their first knives, slingshots, or
BB guns (or all three, if you were a very good little girl

or boy). Girls in South Texas celebrate their fifteenth birthdays with *quinceañeras,* extravagant coming-of-age parties (think $20,000 dresses and Hummer limos) that rival the pomp and circumstance of the average wedding. During Homecoming, high schoolers exchange mums, a mutant cousin of the corsage that is essentially a freakishly large, flowered, jeweled, and beribboned pin that weighs as much as the teenager wearing it.

But since rites of passage occur during all moments that you cross a metaphorical threshold that leads to greater knowledge about a culture, they can continue well into adulthood. Often, experiential immersion is the only way to gain the wisdom a rite of passage is meant to impart, whether that means attending cultural and historical events like Fiesta or Juneteenth; learning specific traditions and customs, like how to fold the flag or build an altar for a deceased loved one; or even surviving an ordeal, like getting cedar fever in the winter.

Becoming a Texan is a lifelong process and isn't simply a matter of checking off items on a list, but there are a few traditions that brand their participants with a bit more authenticity.

★ ★ ★

HANDLE THE TEXAS FLAG

There's no better way to showcase your pride than by flying the Lone Star flag in front of your house on state holidays, but the true Texan knows a thing or two about how to do it correctly. The guidelines for handling the flag were first adopted in 1933 by the Legislature, and they are similar to those for the US flag: it should be flown at night only if it is clearly illuminated; it should never touch the ground; and a tattered flag should be destroyed, preferably by burning. You won't get fined for breaking these rules, but be mindful that you could lose the respect of your friends. "We get calls all the time from people reporting their neighbors," says David Sauceda, who has served as assistant sergeant at arms in the House of Representatives, the office responsible for the flags that fly over the Capitol in Austin.

Rules for Flying the Flag
- When displaying the flag horizontally, the white stripe must be on top, with the blue stripe to the observer's left. (Fly the flag upside down only to signal distress.)
- When hanging the flag vertically, the blue stripe should be uppermost, and the white stripe should be to the observer's left.
- When flying the US flag and the Texas flag from adjacent poles, the US flag should be to the observer's left (though it is recommended that both flags be at the same height).

Rules for Folding the Flag
In 2009 state senators Judith Zaffirini and Leticia Van de Putte sponsored legislation on how to fold the flag. Here are the proper steps:

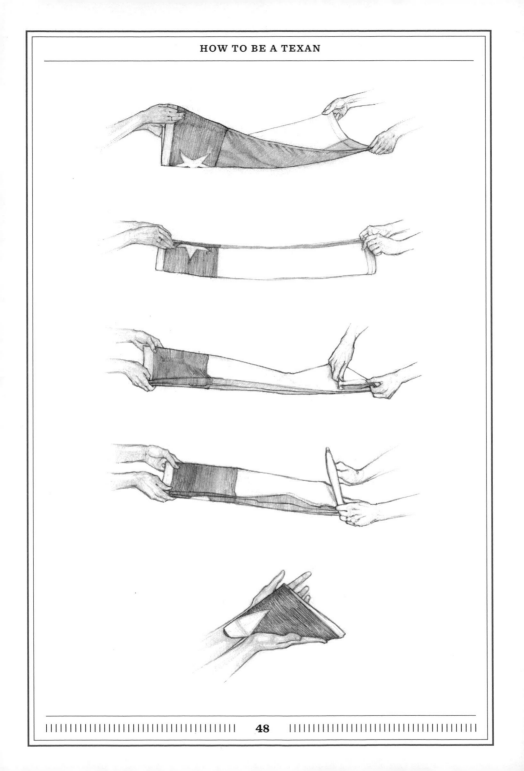

1. Fold in half lengthwise, with the red stripe facing up.
2. Fold in half lengthwise again, with the red stripe concealed on the inside of the fold.
3. With the star facing the ground, fold a corner of the white stripe over to form the edge of a triangle, then continue folding to the opposite end.
4. Tuck in the edge to secure. The flag will be shaped like a triangle, with part of the star showing.

★ ★ ★

TAKE A BLUEBONNET PHOTO

The arrival of springtime in Texas is heralded not by the first shoot of green poking out of the earth, but rather by the sudden eruption of the violet-blue hue of bluebonnets blanketing fields and lining highways. Five species of bluebonnets share the honor of being our state flower, but it is the *Lupinus texensis* that enjoys the greatest celebrity. The showy flower inspires artists of all stripes to replicate its fine and stately detail. And every spring, thousands of babies, toddlers, dogs, newly engaged couples, longtime spouses, and every grouping in between pose in roadside patches of bluebonnets for photos, a tradition nearly every Texan has endured at least once.

But as any amateur shutterbug will tell you, it's notoriously difficult to capture the flower on film. The bloom's vibrant colors look washed-out; the petal's delicate details are lost in a blur. "The flowers are small," says Kenny Braun, a professional photographer based in Austin. "If the wind is blowing or it's the wrong time of day, you won't get a flattering photo." So before you drive

to the country in search of a prime patch of wildflowers, learn the proper technique to ensure that you return home with something picture-perfect.

Setting

Wildflowers bloom in late March and April, months with unpredictable weather. Check the forecast and avoid windy or cloudy days. When the elements align, bluebonnet meccas like Burnet and Ennis explode with color (and crowds), so explore roads less traveled to find pristine fields. When you discover a picturesque spot, check for "No Trespassing" signs before plopping down.

Lighting

Morning between eight and ten is best, but late bloomers can snap some good shots after four or during the "magic hour," the hour or so before the sun sets. (There is also a morning "magic hour," that small window of time soon after the sun rises.) Don't be afraid to experiment with your light source: Stand with the sun behind you, at a forty-five-degree angle, or allow it to backlight your subject for an ethereal look. "Use the camera's flash to help fill in shadows," Braun advises.

Gear

Charge your digital camera and pack an extra memory card. If you use an old-fashioned 35mm, stock up on low-speed film. For both types of cameras, try lower ISO settings, or film speeds, for higher-quality photos, but bring a tripod mount; it steadies the equipment to capture a crisp image. Extreme photographers may want to invest in a polarizing lens filter. "It accentuates the blue in the flowers and sky," Braun says.

Composition

For portraiture, compose a natural frame for your sweethearts and kiddos by incorporating trees, hay bales, or fences. Also try alternative perspectives, from wide angles—including the surroundings and the sky—to close-ups. Practiced photographers might vary the depth of field by changing f-stops. "Small numbers, like f/2.8, produce a shallow depth of field for a selective focus, and large numbers produce lots of focus depth," Braun says. "And when all else fails, shoot the heck out of everything to give you more images to choose from."

★ ★ ★

ATTEND FIESTA IN SAN ANTONIO

Texans know how to throw a party. Consider the galas, luncheons, and lavish soirees hosted by our high-society personages like Joanne King Herring, who, before she was played by Julia Roberts in *Charlie Wilson's War*, entertained a Middle Eastern guest by turning her Houston mansion into a sultan's palace. Or Carolyn Farb, another Houston socialite, whose fundraiser-cum-celebration for local newscaster Marvin Zindler's seventy-fifth birthday featured forty valet parkers wearing white wigs styled in Zindler's signature coif and replicas of the blue sunglasses the journalist was famous for wearing on air.

But every April, San Antonio hosts what could easily be considered the state's most epic party: Fiesta. In its 125-plus-year history, Fiesta San Antonio has grown from a single parade (the Battle of Flowers, a celebration honoring the heroes of the Alamo and Battle of San Jacinto) into an annual eleven-day citywide festival that has an astounding economic impact of more than $280 million. With more than one hundred events on the schedule, the opportunities for fun are legion. To survive this marathon of activities, keep the following party tips in mind.

Parade Around

With so many enticing events to attend, first-time Fiesta-goers often suffer from eyes-too-big-for-stomach syndrome, so before you gorge on festivities, be sure you leave room for Fiesta's three major parades.

The Battle of Flowers Parade, held on the second Friday, is Fiesta's oldest event and largest parade, drawing more than 350,000 attendees, so get there early to nab a primo spot.

The River Parade, put on by Texas Cavaliers, a local charity organization, is "where the floats actually 'float'" down the San Antonio River.

And the climactic finale to the festivities is Fiesta Flambeau, a.k.a. The Night Parade, where more than 500,000 people line up like expectant flies drawn to the literal brilliance of dancers, band members, horses, cars, and floats covered in millions of twinkling lights in an electric spectacle that would put Clark Griswold's Christmas decorations to shame.

Other Requisite Events
Fiesta Oyster Bake (with 100,000 of the bivalves served, you're sure to get some); the carnival (fun for the whole family); A Night In Old San Antonio (a four-night celebration of food and drink held in historic La Villita); and the King William Fair (no days-long festival is complete without funnel cake).

Know the Court
Each year, the organizers of Fiesta choose a royal court to represent the city during the festivities. Be sure to pay your respects.

In Fiesta's early days, there were various kings, including King Selamat and King Omala ("tamales" and "Alamo" spelled backwards, respectively). Today, the Texas Cavaliers select King Antonio, who "reigns over the merriment."

The crowning of El Rey Feo (the Ugly King) is rooted in tradition borrowed from medieval times, when the people selected one of their own to be king for a day. Today he earns his crown by raising funds for the Rey Feo Scholarship Committee.

If there is a king (or two), there must surely be a queen. The Queen of Fiesta and her twenty-four duchesses (twelve from San Antonio and twelve visiting) serve for one year. When the court makes appearances during Fiesta, onlookers scramble to get a glimpse of their ornate dresses that cost up to $50,000. (Also, during the Battle of Flowers Parade, locals always yell at the princesses to "show us your shoes!" which range from tennis shoes to cowboy boots and flip-flops, a stark contrast to the elaborate gowns.)

Other Royal Positions
The Reina de la Feria de las Flores (chosen alongside El Rey Feo); Miss Fiesta San Antonio and the Fiesta Teen Queen; the Charro Queen; and The Queen of Soul, a representative from the African-American community.

Eat, Drink, and Be Merry
Fiesta is, in many ways, no different than any other festival, but there are some traditions unique to the celebration that round out a true Fiesta experience.

Indulge in the Fiesta diet. If it's served on a stick or in a paper cone, order it. Drink plenty of Lone Star (Light, if you insist on counting calories), and stack your cups as a badge of honor to show how much you've imbibed (and to warn others of your alcohol intake).

Wear a flower crown. These colorful wreaths made of paper flowers add vibrancy and festivity to the occasion, and can be homemade or purchased at various booths at the fair.

Crack *cascarones* on someone's head. Starting basically the day after Fiesta ends, locals begin saving intact, empty egg shells (poke a small hole in the narrow end and a larger hole on the wider end, blow the insides out, and fill with confetti) to make next year's batch of cascarones, a.k.a. confetti eggs. Smash these little confetti bombs (gently) on someone's head to blow off a little steam and get a good laugh.

Collect Fiesta medals. Businesses and organizations—from the public library system to the San Antonio Spurs—design and cast medals to commemorate the year. A bountiful collection proves you've made the most of Fiesta.

★ ★ ★

CELEBRATE JUNETEENTH

On June 19, 1865, Major General Gordon Granger, the Union's newly appointed commander of the Department of Texas, stood at the balcony of Ashton Villa, a three-story Italianate-style house in Galveston, and delivered the nearly three-year-old news of a proclamation that had yet to reach our isolated state. Reading General Order Number 3, Granger announced, "The people of Texas are informed that, in accordance with a proclamation from the Executive of the United States, all slaves are free." The black men and women in attendance—representing the more than 250,000 slaves in Texas—erupted into cheers and celebration. The next year, freedmen organized the first of what would become an annual tradition to observe the end of slavery: Juneteenth.

For years, celebrations of Juneteenth (a portmanteau of "June" and "nineteenth") were largely localized to Texas. Before desegregation, black communities in a number of towns and cities—like Austin, Mexia, and Houston—purchased land and converted the grounds into "Emancipation Parks," to celebrate the day. The informal holiday experienced a lull during the civil rights movement, but gained traction and more national prominence in 1980, the year after Governor William P. Clements, Jr. signed legislation drafted by representative Al Edwards, of Houston, designating Juneteenth a state holiday, making it the first official black holiday in US history.

Celebrations vary from community to community, but every Texan should travel to Galveston—a place that has a long and storied history for black Texans, including being home to the first black high school, first public library for African Americans, and first black heavyweight champion of the world—and observe this very unique and Texas-centric holiday at least once. This itinerary is by no means comprehensive (events typically span the week or the month preceding June 19 and include ticketed galas and balls), but it serves as a small start to commemorating Juneteenth.

Morning
Gather outside of Ashton Villa and listen to a reading of the Emancipation Proclamation. It is typical that after the reading, the assembled group will often pray and sometimes join together in song—"Lift Every Voice and Sing" is a popular hymn performed during Juneteenth celebrations.

Afternoon
Specific events vary from year to year, but the Annie Mae Charles Juneteenth Picnic is an annual mainstay. This family-friendly and open-to-the-public picnic features food, drinks, and a reading of the Emancipation Proclamation.

Travel roughly twenty blocks north, to the Old Galveston County Courthouse, where historians will stage a replica of what was the campsite of the Buffalo Soldiers. Actors dressed in period Army uniforms reenact the lives of those stationed at this site before General Granger arrived to give General Order Number 3.

Evening

The culminating event of Juneteenth in Galveston is undisputedly the long-planned parade. A grand marshal leads a trail of mounted horsemen, jubilant marching bands, and elaborate and ornate themed floats sponsored by local social organizations and businesses through the heart of the island, ending near the seawall. Standing along the edge of the island makes one appreciate that though the news was slow to travel to far reaches of America, it's important to celebrate that it came at all.

★ ★ ★

GO TO A STAR PARTY

Out in the Davis Mountains of Far West Texas, as you drive on to a road called Dark Sky Drive, nearly 6,800 feet above sea level, you'll see a smattering of white-and-silver domes dotting the skyline atop Mount Locke and Mount Fowlkes. These are the telescopes of the McDonald Observatory, the University of Texas's astronomical research facility, purposefully situated in the darkest contiguous skies of the continental United States. In its long history, over seventy-five years, the observatory has discovered the first evidence of water on Mars, bounced a laser off of the moon, and spotted the most powerful supernova to date, a star explosion that was one hundred billion times brighter than our sun.

This is all thanks to William Johnson McDonald, a banker from Paris (Texas, that is), who bequeathed a large sum from his vast fortunes to the university. His gift was meant for UT—which had no astronomy department at the time—to build an observatory that would promote "the study of Astronomical Science" by both professionals and the public. Part of that outreach and accessibility to the public is the Observatory's thrice-weekly Star Parties. Each year, thousands of people travel from all over the world to gaze at the more than 100 billion stars in our Milky Way and all that our universe has to offer. "There's just something about the dark nighttime sky that never ceases to thrill me," astronomer Bill Wren once told *Texas Monthly*. "We're raising generations of people in and around our major population centers who have never seen a dark sky."

Below, some other tips to make the most of a trip to this far-flung part of America, where the nights are often clear and always dark.

Know Before You Go . . .

If the party's still on. Before visiting, call the Frank N. Bash Visitors Center to be sure they are open and hosting a Star Party that night.

Reservations are required. Before you drive all the way out to a desert in the middle of nowhere, you must get tickets to the event.

The forecast. In this part of Texas, nights can get chilly, even in the summer. Dress appropriately.

That the phase of the moon could matter. A full moon casts a lot of light, while a new moon allows for better stargazing. They're both fine experiences, but lots of people prefer to go during a new moon or the phases before or after.

To leave your phone behind. The light pollution from your screen adulterates the experience.

That your eyes need to adjust. Before looking through binoculars or the telescopes, allow your eyes five to ten minutes to fully acclimate to the night sky.

* * *

BUILD A DÍA DE LOS MUERTOS ALTAR

Every November 2, known as the Day of the Dead or All Souls' Day, Hispanics across the Southwest transform grave sites, offices, and corners of their homes into vibrant memorials for their deceased loved ones by assembling multitiered *ofrendas*, or altars. "The day is devoted to the departed, and an altar pays special tribute," says Malena Gonzalez-Cid, the executive director of Centro Cultural Aztlan, a nonprofit that has organized San Antonio's largest Día de los Muertos celebration for thirty-plus years. Altars are also meant to welcome returning spirits, so they include both personalized and traditional elements—including several dating to the Aztecs—that will guide an honoree on his journey from the land of the dead. Include these items to offer a proper reception:

- A large photograph of your loved one is the centerpiece. Smaller, informal snapshots can adorn the lower levels.
- Water or, more typically, fruit punch is served to refresh a spirit after his or her journey.
- Pan de muerto, or "bread of the dead," is a sweet treat. Found at most panaderías, the round loaf is topped with a skull and crossbones.
- Salt, a symbol of purification, is for the dead to season the food you've offered him or her.
- The deceased's favorite knickknacks, food, or tools (if your loved one was a barber, for example, a straight razor, foam brush, and scissors) create a familiar and welcoming setting.
- *Cempasuchitl*, the Aztec name for marigolds, grow and wilt quickly, reflecting the fleeting nature of life. Their aroma helps lure a spirit back.
- *Papel picado* serves as a colorful and meaningful trim: Black represents death, purple means grief or mourning, pink is for celebration, white symbolizes hope, and yellow stands in for the sun.
- Four candles at the top represent the cardinal directions and provide a lighted path to this world.
- Sugar skulls, or *calaveras*, add a lighthearted touch— for both the dead and the living.
- Burning copal is a holdover tradition from the Aztecs, who used the incense as an offering to the gods. It is still used in Catholic funeral masses.

★ ★ ★

SURVIVE CEDAR FEVER

While Texans might not typically be snowbound in the winter months, another natural phenomenon keeps us seeking the safety of a carefully controlled indoor environment: cedar season. Immunologists refer to Central Texas as one of the allergy capitals of America because all year long, people in this strip of the state sneeze, snort, and sniffle in attempt to expel the fungus, mold spores, ragweed, and grass stuck in our snouts.

Due to our prolonged growing season and temperate climate compared to other parts of the state—few freezes, few fires to burn off brush—the area is a perfect petri dish for these allergens to thrive. The most vilified of the bunch? The pollen of the mountain cedar. Each year from December to February it rears its heinous head and deploys a chemical weapon that can fell even the strongest individuals.

If the *Juniperus ashei* is the devil—as some may curse during the height of its mating season—its pitchfork of misery is many-pronged. The trees greedily slurp up our most precious commodity, drinking up to thirty-five gallons of water a day. Their off-the-chart pollen counts (especially high after rainy years) waft over the Hill Country, a dirty orange cloud that hangs low until it falls and coats trees, cars, and every still object in sight. And, if you want to be churlish about it—which, after your fiftieth sneeze of the day, you do—cedars are downright ugly.

So what is one to do? If injecting yourself with antivenom is the cure for snakebites, it should only be fair that a shot of gin made from the berries of this juniper variety should cure the allergy that ails ya. Alas, that liquor is made with the cedar tree's relative, *Juniperus communis*. However, there are other remedies, from the homeopathic to the medically invasive.

- Start with the basics and wash your face, your clothes, your pillowcases, your kids, your kid's hair and faces, your dogs, your cats, your curtains, your baseboards . . . basically, anything that might track the pollen into your house and then retain it.
- Move on to saline nasal washes to clear your passages of any offending dander or unwelcome allergens. Then inoculate the area with over-the-counter nasal sprays.
- Take a daily allergy pill.
- If you're still bothered, seek professional help. Make an appointment with an allergist and get on a regimen of immunotherapy shots. A doctor may prescribe stronger antihistamines and a corticosteroid nasal spray.
- If all of that fails, follow the path of J. Frank Dobie. The famed man of Texas letters was so beset by seasonal allergies, he routinely requested a leave of absence from his post as a means to escape the area. Total retreat from a foe that remains entrenched for months might seem to be a severe measure, but we have seen the enemy and he is—*achoo!*

★ ★ ★

SHOOT A .22

Numerous rites of passage dot the path to becoming a true Texan—riding a horse, having your picture taken amongst the bluebonnets—but few are as iconic as learning to fire a rifle. Although there are a variety of types, beginners often train with a .22 caliber. "That's because there's minimal recoil, and the gun and its shells are relatively inexpensive," says Terry Erwin, a former hunter education coordinator for Texas Parks and Wildlife.

When you use any firearm, always be cautious: Point the muzzle in a safe direction, treat the rifle as if it were loaded at all times, and set up an adequate backstop behind your target (bullets can travel up to a mile and a half). Also wear ear and eye protection; the blast from a .22 can reach 130 decibels, and in rare cases the gun can misfire.

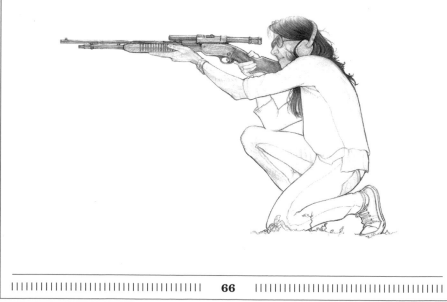

1. Place the butt of the rifle in the pocket between your shoulder and collarbone. Comfortably hold the forearm of the rifle with your nondominant hand.
2. Position your body at a forty-five-degree angle to the target. Plant your feet roughly shoulder-width apart or crouch to hold yourself steady.
3. Put your finger on the trigger only when you are ready to fire. Take a breath, let it about halfway out, hold it, and then gently squeeze—don't slap—the trigger.
4. Erwin advises beginners to load and shoot single bullets (instead of a magazine). To load a bolt action, raise the bolt, then pull it back as far as it will go, place a bullet into the chamber, slide the bolt forward, and lock it.
5. To aim, adjust the firearm so the front sight (a straight piece of metal at the end of the barrel) falls in the V of the rear sight (a smaller piece of metal with a notch in the middle). Line up the front sight just above the spot you are aiming at.
6. Because .22s are short-range rifles, Erwin recommends standing at a maximum distance of 75 yards from the target, but beginners should start between 25 and 30 yards away.

★　★　★

FURTHER READING

Abernethy, Francis Edward, Patrick B. Mullen, and Alan B. Govenar. *Juneteenth Texas: Essays in African-American Folklore*. Denton, TX: University of North Texas Press, 1996.

Simpson, Mrs. Willard E. Jr. "Fiesta San Antonio." Handbook of Texas Online, June 12, 2010. https://tshaonline.org /handbook/online/articles/lkf02.

Tend the RANCH

There's a vastness here and I believe that the people who are born here breathe that vastness into their soul. They dream big dreams and think big thoughts, because there is nothing to hem them in.

Conrad Hilton

The Texas identity is inextricably linked to our connection to the land. And for good reason. For the better part of the state's history, the majority of Texans lived in rural areas. More than half of the state's population lived in the country until 1940, which means generations of families cared for their piece, loving it, fighting it, and attempting to tame it, control it, and wrestle it into submission. And even though the demographics have substantially shifted—roughly 88 percent of Texans live in metropolitan areas now—that bond with the land remains unbroken.

It also helps that there's a certain majesty about our terrain. The high plains of the Llano Estacado in the Panhandle sees a drop of up to 1,000 feet at the Caprock Escarpment, a geographical feature that includes the Palo Duro Canyon, the second-largest canyon in the United States. The Llano Estacado gives way to a swath of rolling lands in North Central Texas, where prairie grasses sway and swirl in the wind, like waves in the sea. Mountain ranges jut from our earth, some so treasured they're part of our National Parks System. The Chihuahuan Desert, the largest in North America, creeps into Far West Texas and presents some of the state's harshest climates. The coastal marshes in Southeast Texas make the land seem almost as permeable as a soft sponge. And large chunks of wilderness remain relatively undeveloped.

With this much variety, it's no wonder that of our 268,596 square miles, we've converted much of it into some of the greatest ranches and farms the nation has ever known. One of the first to capture the nation's imagination was the XIT Ranch, a three-million-acre spread in the Panhandle that, at its height in the late 1800s, operated more than 150,000 head of cattle roaming on ninety-four pastures divided by 1,500 miles of fencing. The JA Ranch next door was co-founded by Charles Goodnight, the most famous rancher in Texas, and it remains the oldest privately owned ranch in the Panhandle. The 535,000-acre Waggoner Ranch, up near the Red River, is the largest contiguous ranch in the world.

And perhaps the most storied ranch in all of America is the King Ranch in South Texas, an 825,000-acre enterprise that is one of the largest cattle operations in the nation.

These ranches all trace their histories back to frontier days, when acquiring that much land was possible, but the appetite for farming and ranching has not waned—in part because when done right, it's a lucrative practice. Texas is home to nearly 250,000 farms and ranches, the most of any state in America. And there's big money in those operations. We lead the nation in cotton production (one-fourth of the total production of the crop in all of America, worth a staggering $1.6 billion) and in cattle value (eleven million head of cattle worth $13 billion).

Ranching as a major industry has existed in Texas for roughly three centuries, dating back to when Spaniards brought livestock with the *entradas* that settled the land. They also brought many of the working procedures still practiced today, and, of course, many of those methods formed the base of the modern-day rodeo. (A few different towns lay claim to hosting the world's first rodeo, but Pecos, Texas, can plant a significant stake by saying it was the first to hand out prizes at its event held on July 4, 1883.)

But for anyone tempted to evoke the romantic notion conjured up by Hollywood that owning a ranch is all about peace and tranquility and surveying the land while watching majestic sunsets from an expansive wraparound porch, you must disabuse yourself of those fanciful notions. Farming and ranching is hard work.

If you raise crops, the soil must be tilled, turned, and tested. Seeds must be planted, watered, fertilized, and the produce harvested. When you sell your bounty, you *might* fetch a market price that yields a slim profit margin (if it turns one at all). Then you have to repeat the process all over again for the next season.

If you keep livestock, the animals must be fed, watered, branded, herded, immunized, birthed when needed, and killed if necessary, among an arm's-length list of other tasks that pop up on any given day.

Even if you keep nothing on your land, there's still general maintenance to be done: fixing fences, paying taxes, dealing with ag extension officers, digging wells, chasing away critters, burning trash, clearing brush, chopping trees, finding water . . . you get the idea. The inexorable to-do list passes from generation to generation, never to be quite completed.

But for those who sign up for this life, that hard work does get noticed. As Theodore Roosevelt once said during a visit to the state, "The Texans are perhaps the best at the actual cowboy work."

★ ★ ★

GO WATER DOWSING

When Texas suffers through a long, blistering summer—which is to say, every summer—the state becomes drier than a piece of gas station jerky. In 2011 it was so hot that planes couldn't take off from airports and train tracks were bent out of shape; then-Governor Rick Perry prayed for a downpour to end the drought; and officials in Llano turned to water dowsing, a.k.a. divining, an ancient practice that uses items such as sticks or rods to find water. "Some urban dwellers may think it sounds like magic beans, but it's common practice around here," Llano's city manager Finley deGraffenried said. And that year, it worked for Llano: one dowser found a well that produced 144,000 gallons per day.

Though skeptics insist that a person's unconscious movements cause the subtle reaction of dowsing tools, believers maintain that intuition and natural forces guide the seeker. Before walking into a field with your equipment, clear your mind and ask a simple question: Where is there a clean, flowing source of water? Focus on the query, and one of these tools might lead you to the answer.

Y-Rod

This forked stick is usually crafted from soft, flexible wood such as apple or willow. With your arms extended away from your body, grip the forked ends of the branch, palms facing the sky, and steady the Y-rod at a forty-five-degree angle. Lightly squeeze the branches and begin

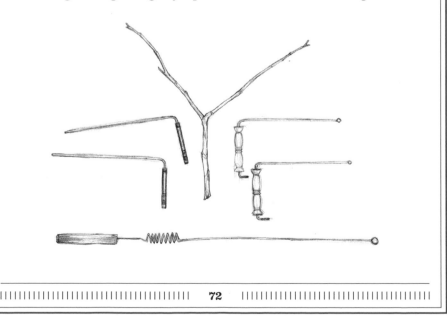

walking. "When the rod responds, it twists and points downward," says Nathan Platt, of the American Society of Dowsers (yes, there is such a thing).

L-Rods

These two bent rods, generally fashioned from steel or copper, are each shaped like the capital letter *L*. The short ends are covered with a plastic or metal sheath, which allows the rods to rotate. Hold the rods in your hands like pistols, and when water is found, they will either cross each other or open wider.

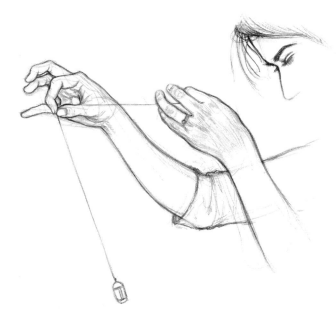

Pendulum

This familiar tool is simply a weight tied to a string. "It can even be something as simple as a paper clip on twine," Platt says. Hold the string with the weight hanging down. Either keep it still or set the pendulum in motion. The weight will respond by moving or changing direction.

Bobber
Crafted specifically for dowsing, the bobber is a thick wire attached to a wooden handle. To use, hold the handle and point the wire at the ground. It will respond to water by moving or changing direction.

★ ★ ★

BUILD A BARBED WIRE FENCE

One of the greatest origin stories in all of Texas history comes by way of the aptly-named fence salesman John W. Gates. In 1876 Gates put on a show of theatrics that could rival a Cirque du Soleil performance, telling people he could capably contain a small herd of ornery cattle in downtown San Antonio. Gates erected a fence in Military Plaza, an arena smack dab in the middle of town, and shocked a gathered crowd as a herd of enclosed Longhorns backed away from eight thin strands of spiky wire.

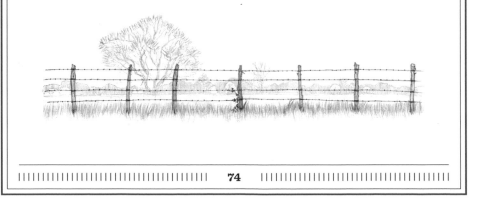

"That was a turning point," says Davie Gipson, the curator of the Devil's Rope Barbed Wire Museum in McLean. "When barbed wire came along, it stopped open-range traveling the way Indians and cattlemen knew it." It also caused some thorny relations: While farmers enjoyed better crop protection, ranchers despised the constricted spaces, and soon range wars (and wire-cutter manufacturers) multiplied. Today, however, barbed wire remains the simplest and most popular way to mark your rightful territory and manage your mooing moneymakers.

The Wire

There are more than 570 patented wire styles, many equipped with fancy barbs, but down-to-earth ranchers use the two- or four-point varieties. Because metal weakens when exposed to fertilizers or elements like humidity and sand, manufacturers offer a range of protective coatings; which one you choose will depend on your needs and your wallet. According to Brian Cowdrey, a veteran fenceman who works for the League City–based American Fence and Supply Company, Class I galvanization, the least expensive, has the thinnest finish and the shortest life span—usually eight to ten years—while Class III has a heavier coating that prevents rust for at least twenty years. A spool generally holds 1,320 feet, and most ranchers opt for twelve-and-a-half-gauge, double-stranded wire.

The Posts

A fence is only as good as its posts. Invest in metal or a durable, treated wood. Or, for an authentic look, repurpose downed trees, like cedar. The typical post measures four to eight inches wide and eight feet long. Since lengths of taut barbed wire exert heavy pressure, take care to anchor your posts well: Holes should be dug at least two feet deep (for extra stability, secure them with poured concrete) and placed roughly eight to fifteen feet apart. "The key to any fence is your corner, or end, posts," Cowdrey says. "You need to brace them so the wire doesn't pull your fence down." Brace each end post using a piece of wood nailed horizontally between it and its adjacent posts, then run a length of wire diagonally between the posts to strengthen the corner.

The Assembly

After reviewing an aerial map of your property and drawing a blueprint of your intended boundaries, install the posts, then lay out the wire along the inside of the perimeter. Fasten your first strand near the top of a corner post. Walk to the next corner and, using a wire stretcher (available at most hardware stores), tighten the line, then staple it to the post there. Next, fasten the wire to each intermediate post. "Don't drive the staple all the way in," Cowdrey cautions. "You want room for the wire to expand and contract." Repeat with each strand, working from top to bottom. "Animals will stick their heads just about anywhere for that next blade of grass,"

Cowdrey says, so make sure you add enough strands to stop them (at least eight for goats, at least four for cattle). You certainly don't want your livestock running amok, a precaution that neighbors—who, as the saying goes, appreciate good fences—will be happy you took.

★ ★ ★

SHOE A HORSE

Wild horses, which can cover up to twenty miles a day, wouldn't think of having their hooves done, but leave it to humans to change all that. "When we domesticated the animal, ten thousand years ago, we restricted its movement," says John Burgin, the owner of the Texas Horseshoeing School, in Scurry. "Now their feet need protection, just like a person's." Optimal maintenance includes regular inspection and cleaning, and reshoeing, which should be done roughly every six to eight weeks. Before grooming, securely tie up your horse, then run your hand down his leg to alert him to square up on the other three. Squeeze the tendon above the ankle, lift the hoof, and begin your pony's pedicure.

1. First clean out any compacted dirt, mud, and manure with a curved tool called a hoof pick. Work from heel to toe with downward strokes, but take care around the frog (the sensitive triangle in the middle of the hoof's underside).
2. The front of the hoof wall should measure between 3 inches and 3¾ inches from the hairline down. If it is too long, cut the excess off with a set of nippers.

Keeping the blades parallel to the bottom of the hoof, start at the right heel and work toward the middle of the toe, trimming evenly. Repeat from the left heel.

3. Use a rasp, which looks like an enormous Microplane grater, to file the hoof until it is level.

4. Place the shoe on the hoof wall and drive a nail into each hole. (The nail should go in at an angle and poke through the front of the wall.) With the nippers, clip the ends of the nails. Then clinch down the metal. Finally, use the rasp to smooth out any rough edges. "You should be able to run pantyhose over the hoof with no snags," Burgin says.

★ ★ ★

CUT THE HERD

When Sam Graves and his twenty-two-year-old bay gelding, Old Hub, beat ten other cowboys to win $150 in the first advertised cutting competition in Haskell in 1898, he could not have imagined how the sport would evolve. Today the National Cutting Horse Association, which hosts the World Championship Futurity in Fort Worth, has more than 20,000 members and pays out more than $40 million to its champions. "Cutting is addictive," says former NCHA president Chris Benedict. "I've never known anyone to try it just once." Though the stakes may be higher today, the challenge remains the same. A horse and rider must separate—or cut—a calf from the herd and work the animal to keep it from returning to the group, a skill used on ranches to brand or doctor cattle. "The horse does all the work," Benedict says with a laugh. "Maybe that's why people like it."

The Rider

It's not easy to be on autopilot while a thousand-pound beast pivots, veers, and breaks from side to side on its own. Once a rider finds a good horse, she develops a relationship with the animal so they both can remain calm and confident in show situations (cattle may not be bright, but they sense uncertainty). Though the horse has been taught to act independently, the rider plays a role in the performance as well. "In cutting, balance is key," Benedict says. The rider has to fight the inclination to lean into turns, and learn to sit upright and still.

The Horse

Nothing is more important than the horse: Offspring of champions can sell for up to $750,000. American Quarter Horses make up more than 90 percent of cutters, primarily because they are stocky, agile, and have a natural desire to compete. Training generally begins at two and continues through the animal's life. "Most of them have day jobs working cattle at the ranch," Benedict says.

The Event

Few have the chance to compete, so while it's likely you'll never step into the arena, it's nice to know what's happening during the show. When a rider crosses the start line, she has two and a half minutes to cut two to three calves out of the herd. Without spooking the cattle, the rider and her horse will approach the pack and choose the first calf. Through some nifty maneuvering, the calf will be coaxed out, and the rider will "throw [her] hand down," or drop the reins. It's at this point that the horse demonstrates its "cow sense." If properly trained, the horse will position itself between the herd and the calf and, holding its head low, lean on its haunches, moving back and forth to keep the calf separated. A rider will work the calf to earn points, then repeat the process. If a competitor loses a calf or stops working the animal mid-cut, the judges penalize her. Scores range from sixty to eighty, with points awarded for style, balance, and horse and rider judgment.

★ ★ ★

ROPE A CALF

Ask a ranch hand how to tell if someone's a good cowboy and he'll say the proof is in his lassoing. The rope has always been "the long arm of the cowboy," writes Midland native John R. Erickson in his book on the subject, *Catch Rope*. Though roping began on the ranch as a way to wrangle stray calves or round them up for branding, it demanded such precision and dexterity—and sparked so much bragging—that it gave rise to a competitive sport. Now a mainstay of rodeos, tie-down roping (it's no longer PC to call it "calf roping") is one of the most highly respected contests at events each year, like the much-revered Fort Worth Stock Show and Rodeo, where contestants try to chase, catch, and immobilize a 250-pound calf in the least amount of time possible.

The Rope

The rope, or lariat, has an eye, or a honda, tied at one end, through which the other end is threaded to form a big loop (four to six feet in diameter). The twenty-five-foot rope is generally a ten-millimeter-thick, three- or four-ply polyester cord (to limit stretching) with a stiffness, or lay, of extra-soft, soft, or firm. To throw, "move your wrist in a counterclockwise direction and swing above your head," advises Stran Smith, of Childress, who was

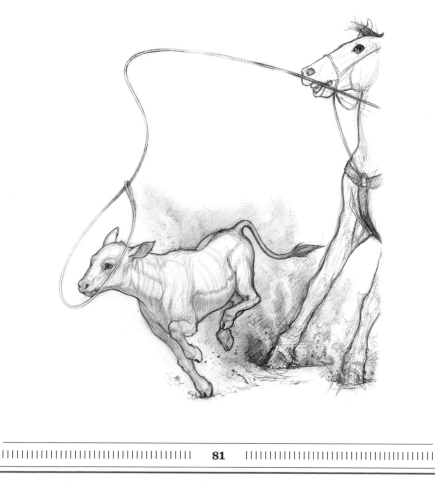

the 2008 Professional Rodeo Cowboys Association world champion tie-down roper. "For the rope to hit your target, don't throw to a broad area. Throw to a specific place—in this case, to the back of the calf's head." Avoid catching other body parts in the lasso, known as "trash in the loop."

The Action
The process during professional competition is as follows: a cowboy enters the box, mounts his horse, primes the lariat (with the loop loose for throwing and the other end tied to your saddle horn), and clenches the piggin' string, a 6.5-foot cord used to tie the calf, firmly in his teeth. He then nods his head to signal the calf's release into the arena and to start the clock. (He won't exit the box before the animal runs or he gets a ten-second penalty.) He'll charge into fifth gear, rope the calf, leap off the horse, throw down the animal, and wrap three legs—generally a front one and the two back ones, instructs Smith—with the piggin' string. The tying method, involving two loops and a knot, is referred to as "two wraps and a hooey." To signal that the work is done, the cowboy throws his hands in the air, a gesture that indicates to the timekeeper to stop the clock. The calf has six seconds to break free; if it escapes, the contestant is disqualified.

The Reward
A typical winning time will fall under 9 seconds; the world record is 5.7 seconds. Clocking the fastest speed can earn someone anywhere from $2,000 to $100,000. (Rodeoing is difficult work that can pay off, so to speak; in 2014 the Wrangler National Finals Rodeo had a total

purse of about $6.375 million.) So while mamas don't want their babies to grow up to be cowboys, the prize money (Trevor Brazile, of Decatur, earned $507,921 in 2010, the single-season record for most money earned) and fame (ESPN has broadcast the NFR from Las Vegas since 1994) sometimes prove too strong a lure.

★ ★ ★

BRAND THE HERD

Why make a lasting impression on your cattle? To fend off cattle rustlers, whose pilfering of literal cash cows is hardly a defunct business (ranchers in Texas lost $4.3 million in livestock in 2011). "Think of branding as a license plate on your car, a means of identification," says Larry Gray, of the Texas and Southwestern Cattle Raisers Association. "A thief will generally pass up branded cattle." That said, you may place heavier stock in your herd's image and well-being: While branding is still prevalent in Texas, some ranches have phased it out because the permanent mark can devalue the hide. And oh, yes, because a burn from a searing hot iron rod is unpleasant.

The Design
Open characters like *C* or *3* guarantee a clear brand; closed ones such as *8* or other too-fancy markings easily blotch. The best brands? Simple symbols that reflect your ranch name and discourage altering by rustlers. Most brand designs stick to no more than four elements—letters, numbers, lines, or circles. The letters

and numbers can be regular or tilted; with legs (marks at the bottom of the character that resemble legs) or wings (squiggles coming off of the top of the letter); or upside down. Lines can run above or below characters, and half- and quarter-circles make the letters or numbers "rock" or "swing." Ranchers often combine two letters or a number and letter to create one symbol. As for dimensions, the brand edges should generally measure three eighths of an inch; anything thinner leaves a deep, narrow mark that gets covered by a winter coat. Entire brand length ranges from four to five inches for cows and three to four inches for calves (to accommodate their growing hides). Always register your customized brand with the local county clerk.

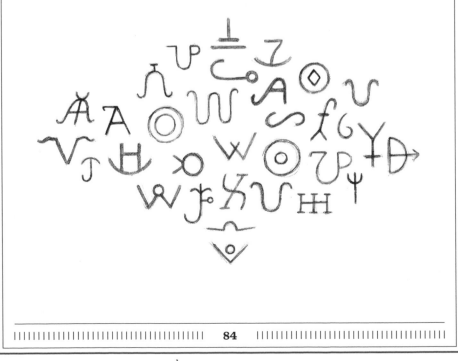

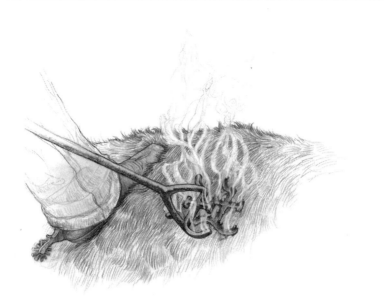

The Method

Hot-iron branding has withstood the test of time (4,000-plus years), making it the most popular technique. For a more visible (and less painful) mark, some ranches employ freeze branding, in which an iron dipped in liquid nitrogen is applied to the hide for about twenty-five seconds. (This destroys the pigmentation and causes the hair to grow back white.) But that process works best on dark-haired animals—and liquid nitrogen ain't cheap. Other identifiers include an ear tag or ear tattoo.

The Application

"First the calf must be immobilized," says Tonnyre Thomas Joe, a South Texas rancher. "Rope and hold it down or maneuver it into a chute." Heat the iron over a wood fire and wait for the brand to turn an ash-gray color (a black iron is too cold, and a red-hot iron can cause the hide to catch fire). Harden your heart and firmly press the iron to the calf's shoulder or hip for three to five seconds, using a rocking motion to cover all points of the brand. Some ranch hands have graduated from the fire pit to electric and propane-heated irons (both better maintain constant temperatures). Never brand a wet hide or you'll wind up with one botched bovine.

★ ★ ★

BARREL RACE

As with most rodeo events, pinpointing barrel racing's exact origin is near impossible. "It probably started out as pretty women on fast horses, but now it's a competitive sport for serious athletes," says Martha Josey, a world-champion barrel racer, Texas Cowboy Hall of Famer, and co-owner of Josey Ranch, a barrel-racing training center in Karnack. This spectator sport, dominated by women, dates back to at least 1948, when thirty-eight cowgirls in San Angelo formed the Girls Rodeo Association—now know as the Women's Professional Rodeo Association—in an effort to buck the rodeo industry's all-male tradition. The WPRA's most popular draw was, and continues to be, barrel racing, a blink-and-you'll-miss-it event in which the fastest time wins.

The Horse
Successful racing requires, above all else, a worthy steed that responds quickly to cues. Key traits include an even temperament, high levels of physical coordination, and of course, a lot of natural ability. Or, as Josey explains in

terms any red-blooded Texan can understand: "A good barrel horse is like a quarterback—a strong athlete who thinks fast and knows how to lead." Most racers choose Quarter Horses, though paints, Appaloosas, and Arabians aren't strangers to the show grounds either. Josey prefers older horses (in the ten- to twenty-year-old range) for their experience, but some competitors train with younger ones (two to three years old) for their energy. While your horse should feel the need for speed, don't hang around the racetrack looking for winners. "All go and no whoa is no fun," Josey says.

The Arena

Three fifty-five-gallon steel barrels are positioned in a triangle pattern. The distance between each drum varies by venue size, but the standard course, as defined by the WPRA, requires ninety feet between the first barrel and the second; 105 feet between the second and the third, as well as the third and the first; and sixty feet between the start line and both the first and second barrels. There must also be at least eighteen feet between the arena fence and barrels one and two, and at least twenty-five feet between the fence and barrel three. The stopping distance, a small stretch in the alleyway between your takeoff point and the official starting line, should be at least forty-five feet. Most important, rodeo officials must maintain a proper surface: too soft or muddy interferes with a rider's time; too hard and slick makes for dangerous running; loosely packed and aerated is *just* right.

The Race

When given the signal, a contestant gallops down the alleyway and crosses the starting line, triggering the timer. Typically the order of barrel turns is right-left-left, creating the well-known cloverleaf pattern (left-right-right is also permissible). Josey recommends approaching the first barrel's left side with an eight-to-twelve-foot "pocket," meaning the space between you and the drum; the exact size of the pocket will depend on the horse. Come through the turn and aim straight toward the second barrel's right side, this time with a narrower pocket—more like six to eight feet. Take the third barrel in the same way and "head home," as the pros say. Negotiate these turns carefully: knock over a barrel and receive a five-second penalty; miss a turn and you get disqualified. (In some associations, you can be penalized simply for losing your hat.) The entire race takes, on average, fourteen to seventeen seconds—because if you aren't making dust, you're eating it.

★ ★ ★

WRANGLE A RATTLESNAKE

With ten species and subspecies of rattlesnakes calling our state home, chances are you'll find yourself face-to-fang with one sooner or later. Most common to West Texas, rattlers like to den up in dry, rocky crevices, but you'll also find them slithering through grass or slumbering under woodpiles. "Essentially, if you're in West Texas, don't sit down until you've checked the

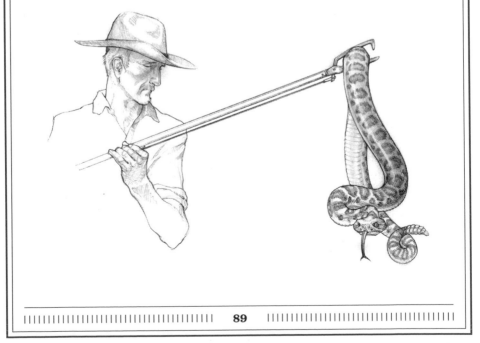

ground within a three-foot radius," says Tom Henderson, a former president of the Sweetwater Jaycees, the organization that hosts the World's Largest Rattlesnake Roundup every year. Why wrangle? The catch-and-release method is more humane than a hoe to the head. (Plus, it makes you look like a badass.)

The Danger
According to the American International Rattlesnake Museum in New Mexico, about eight thousand bites from venomous snakes are reported in the United States each year. But don't say your Hail Marys just yet: Less than one percent result in death. A rattlesnake will usually warn you before it strikes with a low-pitched and unmistakable rattling. (The rattle forms from shed skin and can be very loud—up to eighty decibels.) It also controls the amount of venom it releases, so nearly half of all first bites are dry. But beware: The more threatened a snake feels, the more poison it injects. Young rattlesnakes are considered the most dangerous, as they have not mastered their venom control.

The Wrangling
Henderson is adamant that you wear the protective clothing when you're traipsing around West Texas—leather boots (hard to penetrate) and long pants (preferably jeans)—in the event that you encounter a snake in the wild. If you do find a snake on your property and want to relocate it away from your home, invest in the right equipment: Professional snake handlers use a pinning hook (a metal rod with a U-shaped end), but amateurs should employ snake tongs, which consist of

a long bar with a handle and a set of jaws on one end. (Both devices are about three feet long, to keep the reptile at a safe distance.) Depending on the snake's length (they range from about forty-eight to sixty inches), use the tongs to grip it around its middle or a third of the way down from its head; this will limit striking range. Note where the snake's mouth is, grab its tail above the rattle, and carefully guide it into a large bucket, clamping down the lid.

The Trophy

If you're going to dispatch the venomous thing, waste not, want not: Have a tanner fashion the skin into a chic accessory, indulge in the delicacy of chicken-fried rattlesnake, or hire a taxidermist to memorialize the snake's last tango. But don't let negative mythology dictate your actions: Snakes, after all, control rodent populations and rodent-borne diseases, so let your bleeding heart beat and release it into the wild. The greatest memento will be the heroic tale of your battle with the beast.

★ ★ ★

FURTHER READING

Dobie, J. Frank. *A Vaquero of the Brush Country: The Life and Times of John D. Young.* Austin: University of Texas Press, 1998. First published 1929 by the Southwest Press.

Klauber, Laurence M. *Rattlesnakes: Their Habits, Life Histories, & Influence on Mankind.* Berkeley and Los Angeles: University of California Press, 1982.

Wittliff, Bill. *Vaquero: Genesis of the Texas Cowboy.* Austin: University of Texas Press, 2004.

Hunting & Fishing

Few people are willing to
believe that a piece of country,
hunted and fished and roamed
over, felt and remembered,
can be company enough.

John Graves, *Goodbye to a River*

If you're willing to go back far enough, you could claim that hunting in Texas has a long history—one that dates back at least 11,000 years. That's roughly the time period when the Clovis people, a prehistoric Paleo-Indian culture that wandered the area now known as eastern New Mexico and into the Texas Panhandle, killed the *Mammuthus columbi,* or the Columbian mammoth, according to some archaeologists. There's no evidence to say this was the first instance of hunting, but when you consider that the prey was a ten-ton ancestor to the elephant and might have been taken down with primitive means and tools, it's certainly one of the more impressive examples of the activity.

Things have changed substantially in the intervening millennia. Foremost, the idea of hunting has evolved, so to speak, from a means of survival into a leisure sport. It's also morphed into a wildly lucrative business: In 2013, 2.7 million hunters and anglers from Texas and beyond spent $4.1 billion for the opportunity to take down big game (big horn sheep, white-tailed deer, javelina, and feral hog), exotics (axis deer, nilgai antelope, aoudad sheep), fowl (turkey, duck, quail, dove, and pigeons), and dozens of fresh- and saltwater fish.

In fact, our hunting grounds are so storied that they attracted one of America's most famous sportsmen: Teddy Roosevelt. During a visit to the state in 1892, he insisted on booking a six-day javelina hunt (he bagged two). Later, in 1905, after he became president, Roosevelt traveled back to Texas for a Rough Riders reunion in San Antonio. After the reunion, he made his way back up through northwest Texas to hunt coyotes in the Comanche Territory in present-day southwest Oklahoma.

And while our twenty-sixth president was a skilled and avid hunter, he was also a dedicated conservationist. He chronicled the near-extinction of the buffalo and made great efforts to save the beast from total annihilation. So perhaps were he alive today, he would be proud of our state's conservation efforts. The Texas Parks and Wildlife Department oversees the rules and regulations that allow for responsible hunting to be sure that we are good stewards of the land, and as a result, certain wildlife populations flourish. Texas is home to nearly 25 million mourning dove, more than 3 million white-tailed deer, 100,000 javelina, and more than 2 million feral hogs (though they have become a nuisance, due to their propensity to disrupt habitats of other animals and decimate crops).

But for all of the success of conservation programs around the state, there are still challenges. Encroaching development of our sprawling cities change local environments, and certain industries adversely affect the proliferation of species. Pesticides are partly to blame for diminished bobwhite quail populations, and paper mills in East Texas have come under scrutiny for affecting the squirrel's habitat.

So while hunting may seem like a counterintuitive measure to sustaining wildlife populations, there have been studies that found a demand for hunting actually acts as an incentive for landowners to introduce and cultivate herds. Which means as long as Texans continue to hunt legally and responsibly, it will be a pastime that could be around for millennia to come.

★　★　★

CUT FOR SIGN

After a harrowing skirmish with the Comanche in 1860, Charles Goodnight cut for sign to track down warriors who had escaped. That practice, in which a person searches for people or animals by "cutting," or studying a section of land for clues, may seem like a lost art of the Old West, but it is still used today. "Ranchers cut for sign to find lost dogs and cattle or to find trespassing animals that could damage their property," says Brad Guile, who lives near El Paso and used the technique when he was stationed at Fort Bliss. Hunters also use the skill to stalk animals.

By identifying subtle changes in the landscape, a person can determine where an animal has been, where it is headed, and how old its tracks are. Start by scouring areas where it would be easy to pick up an animal's trail—dirt roads, riverbanks, and open areas with little vegetation—and look for these indicators.

Regularity
A general rule is to look for patterns created by lines, circles, or other marks unique to your animal. "Think about the traffic in the area," Guile says. For instance, if you are looking for a pony and live near herds of cattle, check the ground for horseshoe marks to find your missing animal.

Flattening
When livestock moves across grass or dirt, it compresses the ground, leaving a visible imprint. Determine the animal's speed and health by examining its prints: running animals leave deep prints with long strides; uneven prints could indicate a limp from an injury. Fresh prints have sharp edges, while the outlines of older tracks will have degraded over time.

Color Change
"As you glance across a field, look for shine, or spots where the sun reflects the ground's color differently,"

Guile says. For example, when an animal tramples grass, it bruises the blades, altering their color. Also, freshly overturned dirt is darker than normal. You can best observe differences in color when the sign is between you and the sun.

Disturbance
Study the landscape for overturned rocks, broken fence posts, snapped branches, or any indication that something has been moved from its original position. Other physical signs to look for are fur tufts on barbed wire or blood trails.

★ ★ ★

TIE A TEXAS RIG

Modern-day bass fishing owes its enormous popularity to two game-changing events. First, in 1949, Nick Creme rocked the angler community with the creation of the

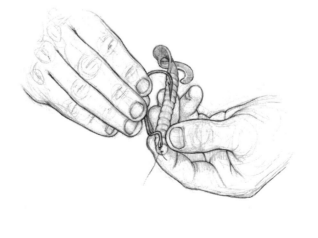

plastic bait worm. Roughly ten years later a fisherman on Lake Tyler, weary of snagging his hooks on submerged timber and vegetation, speared a plastic worm on his hook in such a way that he securely anchored the worm and buried the barb. The Texas rig was born. Why was this technique so revolutionary? "Before the Texas rig was invented, lures had exposed hooks," says Wayne Kent, the president of the Tyler-based Creme Lure Company. "If you fished near a brush pile, the hook could burrow in the wood and cause you to lose the lure." Now a fisherman can cast his bait into those wooded spots that bass love and know he'll reel in more than a blue-ribbon branch. To tie a Texas rig, you'll need three things: a plastic worm (or your preferred creepy-crawly), a hook, and a bullet weight. After you thread the bullet weight and tie the hook to a line, follow these five simple steps.

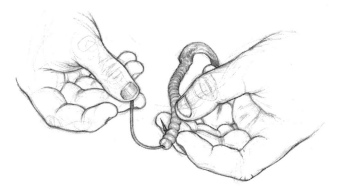

1. Insert the barbed end of the hook into the tip of the worm's head. Push it down about a quarter of an inch until the barb pokes out.

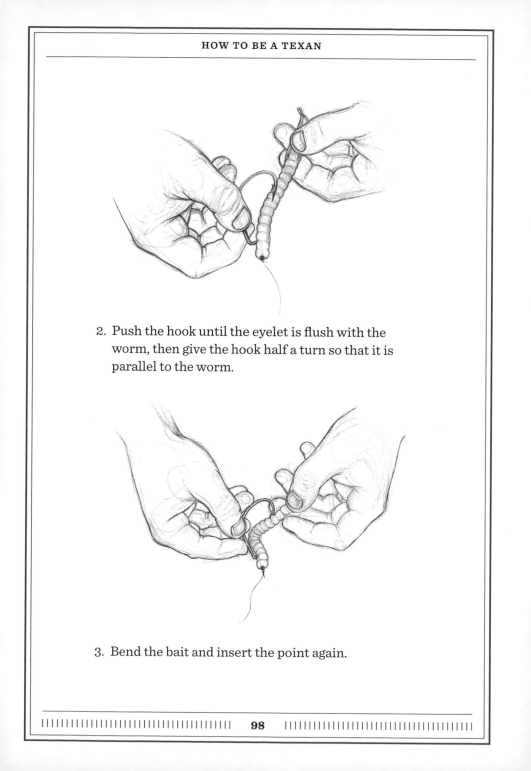

2. Push the hook until the eyelet is flush with the worm, then give the hook half a turn so that it is parallel to the worm.

3. Bend the bait and insert the point again.

4. The barbed end should now rest flat against the worm, which is impaled by the hook at two different points.

5. Lift the worm between the entry points and bury the barbed end until the point is slightly embedded. Now you're ready to land a Texas-size trophy.

★ ★ ★

NOODLE FOR CATFISH

Catching a catfish with your bare hands has been a tradition passed down for generations, but it has only been legal in Texas since September 1, 2011. That's when Governor Rick Perry signed a bill that officially permitted noodling. "No one knows why it was illegal," said Houston representative Gary Elkins, the author of the legislation, though some critics worry that the practice hurts the catfish population, because it occurs during the spring and summer spawning seasons. "The fish nest in holes along riverbanks to defend their eggs from intruders," says Bradley Beesley, the Austin-based director of the documentary *Okie Noodling*. The hiding spot makes them easy prey, but "when attacked," Beesley says, "they bite."

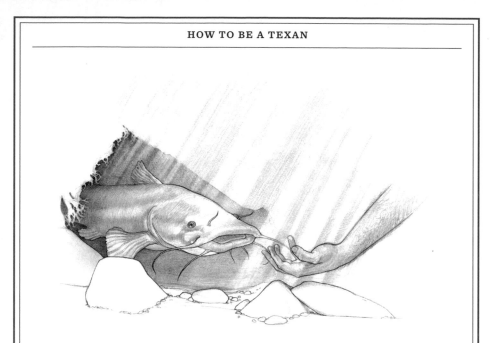

The Nest

Though the creeks and lakes of North and East Texas are rich with flathead catfish, the hardest part about noodling is finding a nest. "It takes people years to cultivate these spots," Beesley says. He advises fishing with a knowledgeable noodler who knows where to find underwater nooks, hollow tree trunks, and other honey holes where the fish hide.

The Catch

Dive down next to the hole and stick your hand in the catfish nest. Since the fish is protecting its eggs, it will react aggressively, so be prepared for it to chomp (no one will think you're a sissy if you wear gloves). Grab the "suitcase-handle-like" lower jawbone, and pull it close to you. If it's a larger fish, you can reach through its gills, but be aware that this will kill the animal. Then thrust your catch toward the surface; your noodling buddy should be ready to help you rassle the fish onto the boat or bank.

The Prize
You'll need more equipment to cook the fish than catch it. Clean and skin the fish, then dip it in a simple corn-meal batter, fry in hot oil until golden brown, and serve with hush puppies.

★ ★ ★

HUNT FOR DOVE

For many hunters, Labor Day weekend is synonymous with the soft coos of the mourning dove. Every year, roughly 350,000 people in Texas are seduced by this avian siren song and are drawn out to harvest about five million of the four-ounce birds—that's about 30 percent of the total number shot in the United States. Why is dove hunting so popular here? "Texas has more dove than any other state," says Corey Mason, who is the director of Region 3 for the Texas Parks and Wildlife Department. "It's an inexpensive, social sport that can be enjoyed by almost everyone." Before you dust off your 12-gauge shotgun, be sure to check the regulations in the region where you'll be hunting. There is statewide daily bag limit (fifteen birds), and the north and central zones enjoy seventy-day seasons. (Regulations can change over time and vary depending on where you hunt. Be sure to visit tpwd.texas.gov for more information on your area's season.)

The Site

Doves can be found all over the state, but according to Tom Stephenson, the owner of the Dallas-based hunting and fishing guide company World Wide Blast & Cast, Central Texas is their primary flyway. For a weekend hunt, lease at least two adjacent fields in a twenty-mile radius so you can move if an area winds up being light on birds, and because a single spot will typically support only two hunts before the birds get wise. The optimal landscape includes seed-bearing plants and bodies of water (to attract feeding doves) and small trees or shrubs (for easy concealment). Morning hunters should set up no later than 6:30 a.m., but "if the birds aren't flying by 7:40, it's time to move," adds Stephenson. Evening shooters will be most successful right before dusk, when the doves return to roost.

The Hunt

For a high-yield hunt, you need three things: appropriate equipment, practiced technique, and total stillness. First, when buying ammo, spring for the good stuff. Most hunters use the less expensive one-ounce No. 8 shells, but Stephenson recommends loading your shotgun with high-brass No. 9 shells (for more punch) and adding a skeet barrel (for wider spread). Second, know how to mount your weapon quickly. "Practice in the mirror so that every time you throw your gun to your shoulder it lands in the same place," says Stephenson. Finally, take a tip from Elmer Fudd: Be vewy, vewy quiet. When a bevy of doves flies by, resist the temptation to stand up and pop off a shot. Remain motionless until the birds cross into your range of accuracy (for most shooters, that's thirty-five yards or less), then in one swift motion, stand, mount your gun, and, keeping your eyes square on the target, lead the birds—that is, aim slightly ahead of their flight pattern—and pull the trigger.

The Bounty

When the birds fall, immediately find your way to them (or send a retrieving dog if you have one trained). Check each downed dove's leg for a band attached by the state: Mason says that thousands of birds can be tagged as a way of tracking their movement and population counts, so you can help the TPWD's research by calling the number on the band. Most hunters breast the doves (cut off the wings and head and separate the breast from the back) in the field, though others return to camp first before processing the birds, especially if they have plans for the whole carcass. Once you fill your bag, it's time to crack a cold beer, fire up the grill, and cook your fresh game the traditional way: wrapped in bacon with a slice of jalapeño. As any dove hunter knows, there's no greater delicacy.

★ ★ ★

BAG A JAVELINA

When Theodore Roosevelt visited Texas in 1892, he booked a six-day javelina hunt. He shot two, but later opined that the best way to dispatch the animal would be by spear. Teddy was on to something. "Because of their poor eyesight, it's easy to close in on javelinas," says David Synatzske, former manager of the Chaparral Wildlife

Management Area, near Cotulla. Found primarily in South Texas, the Trans-Pecos, and the Edwards Plateau, javelinas travel in packs and thrive in environments with heavy white brush or prickly pear, their favorite snack. Adult males can weigh fifty-five pounds and have two-inch-long canines. (When threatened, they clack their teeth, which sharpens their tusks and alerts the herd.) To compensate for their bad vision, they have a heightened sense of smell, so stay downwind when hunting. Unlike those white-tailed deer that trophy hunters are so fond of, javelinas know how to fight back.

Baiting
While purists prefer unaided stalking, baiting a *sendero*—a South Texas term for roads and open paths—with shelled corn will attract a pack. Also scatter bait near watering holes, advises Jerry Gonzalez, the owner of the Laredo-based outfitter, Pedernal Bowhunts.

Weapon
Old-school hunters generally opt for the traditional bow, says Gonzalez, but beginners do well with a compound bow, a modern contraption that aids in accuracy and speed. Use arrows with one-inch broadheads, which are tips specifically designed for hunting big game.

The Hunt
Javelinas can be hunted year-round in fifty counties, but remember that game animals can be harvested only during the day. After prearranging for a lease or coordinating with an outfitter, place corn on the ground early and wait nearby, concealed in the brush if possible.

When the herd approaches, single out a javelina, draw your bow, and aim directly behind the shoulder. After the pack disperses, inspect for a clean kill and field-dress the animal. Skin and break down the javelina when you have access to clean water.

The Trophy
Javelina meat makes a good meal and tastes best slow-cooked, smoked, or jerkied. Or intimidate nearly anyone with a fearsome shoulder mount or a bleached skull.

★ ★ ★

FIELD DRESS A DEER

So you've downed your first buck of the season. Before you start celebrating and, like Bubba Blue with shrimp, begin imagining all the ways you'll prepare the meat (venison sausage, venison chops, venison enchiladas, venison schnitzel, bacon-wrapped backstrap), remember that you've got some dirty work to do. "The minute the animal dies, it's starting to decay," says James C. Kroll, a.k.a. Dr. Deer from the Outdoor Channel (and currently professor emeritus of forest wildlife management at Stephen F. Austin State University). "The sooner you get the insides on the outside the better."

Before setting about your task, first things first: tag your kill (failure to do so will result in a sizable fine from the game warden). Turn the deer so it's lying on its back, then wipe its belly free of debris. If this is your first time on the job, there's no need to slit the animal's throat; the deer will sufficiently bleed out in the field-dressing process. Now you're read to do the dirty work. (Warning: this is a graphic process and is described as such.)

1. Field dressing starts at the tail end. Most hunters split the pelvis for access to the rectal tract, but you can bypass this step if you aren't comfortable wielding a buck knife through the thick bone. With your paring knife, cut three or four inches deep around the anus—"It's like coring an apple," says Kroll—all the while being careful not to puncture the bladder (perforating it won't ruin the meat, but, says Kroll, "it will give it an off flavor"). Be sure to separate

all of the connective tissue from the body, then tie the anus off.

2. Move up the body and stand with legs on either side of the animal, facing toward its hind legs. Starting just below the breastbone, pierce the hide and abdominal wall with the paring knife. (If you're looking to add an impressive mount to the trophy room, your cuts should never stray above the breastbone, to preserve the cape.) When making this incision, be careful to not go too deep or you risk rupturing the rumen (a large, white stomach chamber), and releasing a putrid green gunk.

3. Create a V-shaped cradle for your paring knife with your index and middle fingers and slowly work the blade (which should face up and away from you) toward the pelvis while pushing down on the intestines with your free hand. Remove the penis and testicles (or, if it's a female, the udder).

4. Push aside the rumen to locate the diaphragm, the thin muscle curtain that runs along the bottom ribs, and trim through it to access the upper part of the deer.

5. Next, reach into the chest cavity, find the esophagus (it's above the heart and feels like a garden hose), and with your free hand, slip your paring knife up to sever it. Pull the esophagus down toward the pelvis, and all the entrails, including the detached rectum, should come right out. If connective tissue impedes progress (and it most likely will), cut through those pieces until the innards are free.

6. Tie the rope around the deer's neck and hang the carcass from a tree to allow the blood to drain (about

ten minutes). Bag the heart and liver—to some, these are good eats—then bury the entrails or put them in a large trash bag to dispose of back at camp. ("Leaving gut piles lying around just attracts predators," says Kroll.) Rinse out the insides with water, then pat dry. The skinning and breakdown of the animal can be done at camp.

★ ★ ★

TAN A HIDE

According to an old wives' tale, every animal has enough brain matter to tan its own hide. While the amateur tanner may not embrace the technique of smearing that grey matter over flesh, rest assured there's more than one way to tan a deer, so to speak. "Professionals often use harsh chemicals and acids," says Durango-based master taxidermist Clay Wagner, who has been working with skins for about thirty years. "But there is a simple and safe way to tan a hide using household items like salt, baking soda, and vinegar." Once the hide has been removed from the animal, it's ready for processing, but be sure to keep the skin in a cool, dry place while working with it.

Scrape
Cut away all the excess meat and fat from the skin with a sharp knife. Then use the serrated edge of a butter knife to scrape the hide. "This part is time consuming," Wagner says. But it is integral to the process.

Salt
Spread the skin out, fur side down, on a flat surface. Completely cover the fleshy surface with salt (not rock salt). "You cannot use too much," Wagner says. Leave overnight. The next day soak the salted skin in clean water for up to two hours, or until the skin is soft.

Soak
"Pickling the skin helps prepare it for tanning and sets the hair," Wagner says. Make a pickle bath in a plastic tub using equal parts distilled white vinegar and water plus two pounds of salt per gallon of solution (a typical deer hide requires about four gallons). Immerse the skin and leave for up to three days, stirring several times per day. Then neutralize the skin by soaking it in a solution made from four gallons of water mixed with two cups of baking soda for up to forty minutes. Rinse in clean water and towel dry.

Slick
Oil the skin to prevent it from cracking or drying out. Using a tanning oil solution, which can be purchased online, evenly coat the flesh side. Fold in half, with the fur side facing out, and let it sit overnight.

Soften
Hang the skin up until it is nearly dry, then work the flesh side over a table edge or wooden sawhorse until the skin is pliable. "The more you work it, the softer it becomes," Wagner says.

★ ★ ★

FURTHER READING

Huser, Verne. *Rivers of Texas*. College Station: Texas A&M University Press, 2000.

Kroll, James C. *A Practical Guide to Producing and Harvesting White Tailed Deer*. Nacogdoches, TX: Arthur Temple College of Forestry and Agriculture, 1994.

Richards, Matt. *Deerskins into Buckskins: How to Tan with Brains, Soap or Eggs*. 2nd ed. Ashland, OR: Backcountry Publishing, 2004.

Telfair II, Raymond C. *Texas Wildlife Resources and Land Uses*. Austin: University of Texas Press, 1999.

6

Cook Like a

TEXAN

Texas does not, like any other region, simply have indigenous dishes. It proclaims them. It congratulates you, on your arrival, at having escaped from the slop-pails of the other forty-nine states.

Alistair Cooke, *Letters from America: 1946–2004*

The pride that Texans bear—that we are of a unique community unlike any other—has been well established. We talk a little differently. We dress a little differently. Our food's a little different. Yet within our borders lie cities and regions separated by hundreds of miles, and, at times, by varying idiosyncrasies and influences. Nowhere is that more evident than at our supper tables. Our state's menu features items derived from the traditional foods of the Cajuns (crawfish, gumbo, and catfish), Germans and Czechs (kolaches, schnitzels, and smoked sausage), African Americans (fried chicken and stewed greens), and, perhaps most intrinsically, Mexicans.

The amalgamation of Texan and Mexican cuisines—Tex-Mex, as the locals call it—belongs wholly and completely to us, a style of cooking that, outside of our boundaries, is often imitated, but never replicated. It emerged in the hardscrabble frontier kitchens of cowboys and vaqueros; its lineage, as with many things here, directly attributable to our days as cattle country. The pioneer cattleman Charles Goodnight made indelible contributions to our culture, chief among them the invention of the chuck wagon (our state vehicle) in 1866. Cowboy groceries of the time ranged toward goods that traveled well, like flour for biscuits and sourdough, lard for cooking, and salt pork and beans for stews. Perishables consisted of what could be foraged during the drive, and chiles, long a staple of Mexican cooking, were ubiquitous. Trail cooks, like the fictitious surly Mexican bandit Bolivar from *Lonesome Dove*, tossed meat with dried chiltepin (our state native pepper) into Dutch ovens (our state cooking implement) to make chili con carne (our state dish), and served the bowl of red with a side of *pan de campo* (our state bread).

During the intervening 150 years, that connection has only strengthened. The 78th Legislature christened tortilla chips and salsa the state snack and the sopaipilla the state pastry (an honor shared with the strudel). *Nopales* are a delicacy made from the roasted pads of the prickly pear cactus (our state plant). The Texas red grapefruit (our state fruit) is largely considered to be the world's best grapefruit, and is grown in the Rio Grande Valley, a predominantly Hispanic part of the state. Hundreds of Texas-themed cookbooks have been published, and every single one of them pays homage to the tradition of Tex-Mex.

Even our markets tailor their inventories to our tastes. Fiesta, a grocery store founded in Houston in 1972, caters to Hispanic consumers and has grown into one of the largest grocery chains in the state, with sixty stores in Texas. H-E-B, a grocery store chain based in San Antonio (and the favorite of many a Texan), operates more than 350 markets, including fifty-one in Mexico. And the chains whose headquarters are based far from Texas, like Randall's (California) and Kroger (Ohio), know that to compete, they need to sell certain staple ingredients—like fresh tortillas and Anaheim peppers— you won't find as readily in their stores in other states.

Our culinary heritage, of course, is more than just Tex-Mex. Nearly as revered as melty cheese enchiladas is the enduring tradition of Central Texas barbecue—specifically brisket. While that dish has long been a staple of the state's menu, wood-smoked brisket has seen a bit of a surge in popularity in recent years. Lockhart, Texas, long reigned as the unofficial capital of Texas barbecue, thanks in large part to the public's devotion to legendary joints like Kreuz Market and Black's Barbecue. For decades, the small town drew a steady stream of hungry hordes that bought meat by the pound. But then allegiances shifted when Aaron Franklin, a pitmaster who trained with the Muellers, a well respected barbecue family from Taylor, Texas, opened a food trailer off of I-35 in Austin. Within a couple of years, Franklin Barbecue was declared the "best barbecue in America" by *Bon Appetit* magazine, and standing in the famously long line to get served has become a nouveau Texas rite of passage. Since then, our capital city's smoked-meats scene has exploded, with pitmasters rivaling rock stars for local celebrity status, no small feat in the Live Music Capital of the World. Franklin's specific contribution to the craft has earned him a James Beard Award (the Oscars of the culinary industry) and spawned an obsession with Texas barbecue that's spread across the nation—and the world.

While Tex-Mex and barbecue certainly evoke much of the passion and praise, not to be forgotten are our small-town cafes. Decades-old family restaurants—like Jake and Dorothy's in Stephenville and the Rock Inn Cafe in Seymour—remain community stalwarts, serving down-home cooking like chicken-fried steak, from-scratch mac-and-cheese, and buttermilk pies. Almost as important to Texas's one-light towns are the Dairy Queens and Sonics, where high school seniors celebrate big wins and farmers treat themselves to sweet treats after a long day riding the combine.

Our culinary legacy isn't all comfort food and generations-old recipes and techniques. For years, there has been an intense reckoning with the future of food occurring in our big cities. A group of innovative chefs in Dallas—like Stephan Pyles and Dean Fearing—helped turn Southwestern cuisine into a global food movement during the mid-eighties. Tyson Cole trained in Japan under sushi masters and brought his skills back to Austin, where, in 2003, he opened the critically acclaimed and award-winning restaurant Uchi. A constant stream of increasingly talented chefs continue to crop up in or flock to Texas, prompting national food magazines like *Bon Appetit, Saveur,* and *Food & Wine,* to single out our food scenes and heap praise on their menus.

★ ★ ★

PORK TAMALES

The first year I threw my own tamalada, I sought my mother's advice beforehand. "Tamaladas are fun," she said, "but not for the host." I shrugged off her warning. When I was growing up, my mom and her six siblings gathered every winter to make tamales, rotating hosting duties from year to year. I remember having to clean my room and help my mom prep food before the thirty or so aunts, uncles, and cousins filled the house. But mostly my memories are of the warm smell of cumin and laughing so hard my cheeks hurt the next day. What's a little work when the payoff is so good?

I promptly invited twenty people to my house—none of whom, I should note, had ever been to a tamalada. I fired off an email telling them to bring fillings and that I'd "take care of the rest." The day before the party, I headed to Fiesta for everything we'd need: fresh garlic, a tub of cumin, a bag of onions, tens of pounds of lard and masa, fatty pork butts for more filling, plus ingredients to make homemade tortillas, borracho beans, and Spanish rice. Oh, and Ziploc bags for the finished tamales. And trash bags. And paper towels. And beer. And ice. And did I have enough spoons, knives, and spatulas to spread masa with? And suddenly, as I stood in the grocery aisle, my mind flashed back to my aunts and uncles, gathered around piles of receipts and a calculator as they divvied up costs and tamales by family. This was not the cheapest of endeavors.

I got home and began frantically trimming corn husks. I boiled, shredded, and seasoned the pork. I washed out coolers. I cleaned the bathroom and mopped my floors. I set up a rented table and chairs. I finally fell into bed at three in the morning, only to rise a few hours later to play hostess (*"¡Bienvenidos, mis tamaleros!* Beer goes in the cooler!"), trainer ("No, no, spread the masa on the *smooth* side of the *hoja*"), and manager to a group whose focus waned as the number of empty beer cans grew ("Please put that down. The filling is for stuffing the tamales, not your face"). Was I having fun? I wasn't sure.

But when we tallied up our bounty at day's end, we'd made nearly one thousand tamales—a right good haul for a bunch of newbies. And they tasted almost as good as the ones I ate as a kid. Best of all, coming together as a group of people who loved one another reminded me of my family—so much so that I've hosted a tamalada every year since. I love how my house smells like warm cumin and I laugh so hard my cheeks hurt the next day.

Yield: Makes about 15 to 18 dozen tamales

THE CHILE PASTE:

20 to 25 ancho chiles, seeds and stems removed
hot water for soaking

Soak chiles in water until soft. In a food processor, grind chiles into a thick paste, adding the soaking water as needed. (To make tamales spicy, also prepare 10 to 12 árbol chiles in the same way.) Set aside to use in filling and masa.

THE PORK FILLING:

> 1 four-to-five-pound bone-in pork butt
> 1 large onion, quartered
> 8 garlic cloves, 4 whole and 3 minced
> ½ to 1 tablespoon salt
> 2 teaspoons pepper
> ½ cup lard
> 2 to 3 tablespoons ground cumin
> ⅔ cup chile paste
> salt and pepper to taste

Cover the pork with water in a deep, heavy pot and boil with onion, whole garlic cloves, salt, and pepper for 90 minutes, or until the meat's internal temperature reaches 160 degrees. Reserve at least 2 cups of pork stock. Remove the pork, allow to cool, then shred the

meat, discarding bone and excess fat. Melt the lard in a large cast-iron skillet over medium heat. Add 2 tablespoons cumin, minced garlic, and ½ cup chile paste and sauté for 3 to 4 minutes, until fragrant. Add shredded meat and enough stock to moisten the mixture. Add remaining chile paste, cumin, salt, and pepper to taste (use árbol chile paste here if you want heat). Set aside. Filling may be prepared a day ahead.

THE MASA:

    1 ten-pound bag fresh masa harina
        (available at Fiesta supermarkets)
    2¼ pounds lard
    ¼ to ⅓ cup pork stock, warm
    2 tablespoons salt, or to taste
    ⅓ cup chile paste, or to taste

On a large work space, knead the lard into the fresh masa for 10 to 15 minutes, adding pork stock a little at a time until the masa is cohesive.

Add salt and chile paste to taste. You can test the masa's readiness by dropping a small amount in a glass of water: if it floats, it is ready to spread.

THE TAMALES:

> 4 to 5 bags dried corn husks
> (available at Fiesta supermarkets)

Soak husks in warm water overnight. When you're ready to start, dry off a handful and place within reach. Take a husk and thinly spread 2 or 3 tablespoons of the masa on its smooth side, covering the bottom two thirds of the

husk (the fat end, not the tapered end). Down the middle of the masa, place about a tablespoon or two of filling. Now fold one side of the husk over the filling, followed by the other side. Then fold the bottom end of the husk toward the exposed edge. Repeat until all the tamales have been made.

Fill steamer pot with water to bottom of basket and bring to a boil. Fill basket with tamales, placed vertically with open end up. Secure lid and steam until masa is firm, about 45 to 60 minutes. They freeze well and can last up to six months. They also make great gifts.

★ ★ ★

CHILI AND FRITO PIE

When Ben Z. Grant, a state representative from Marshall, persuaded the 65th Legislature to make chili the official state dish in 1977, he had history on his side. Many people believe that chili con carne was invented in San

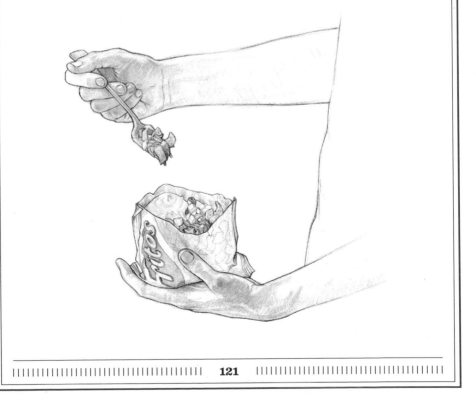

Antonio during the late nineteenth century by women called chili queens, who cooked it over open flames and sold it to soldiers and tourists. Although countless variations exist, the one thing you'll never find in the ingredient list for a legit bowl of Texas red? Beans. "You can't cook them with the chili, because the chemistry isn't right," says Kathleen Tolbert Ryan, the daughter of renowned chili expert Frank X. Tolbert and co-owner of Tolbert's Restaurant in Grapevine, which sponsors the Original Terlingua International Championship Chili Cookoff. But if you decide to add them, we'll never tell.

Yield: Makes 6 to 8 servings of chili

> 1 tablespoon vegetable oil
> 2 pounds lean ground beef
> ½ white onion, chopped
> 2 to 4 minced garlic cloves
> ⅓ to ½ cup ancho chile paste (see recipe on page 116)
> 1 tablespoon dried oregano
> ½ tablespoon salt, to taste
> 1 tablespoon cumin
> 1 tablespoon cayenne pepper
> ½ teaspoon cinnamon (optional)
> 2 tablespoons masa harina or cornmeal
>   (for thickening)
> One 8-ounce can of tomato sauce
> One 12-ounce dark beer, like Shiner Bock
>   or Negra Modelo

In a large pot, brown the meat in the vegetable oil. Remove the ground beef with a slotted spoon, set aside, and cook the onions seven to ten minutes in the remaining fat, until translucent (add vegetable oil, if necessary).

Place meat back into the pot with the cooked onions. Add the rest of the remaining ingredients (except the masa harina) and as much water as needed to keep meat from burning (about 2 inches of liquid above the meat).

Bring to a boil, then simmer for 30 minutes. Taste and adjust seasoning, if necessary. Return to a boil, then cover and simmer for 45 minutes. Stir occasionally and skim off grease.

Add masa harina to thicken, if needed. Simmer another 15 minutes or so, until the chili is your preferred consistency.

TO ASSEMBLE A SINGLE-SERVING FRITO PIE:

Split open a two-ounce bag of original Fritos, and tump in a healthy scoop of chili. Top with a few big pinches of grated cheddar cheese and a small fistful of finely-diced white onion. (If you're feeling fancy, add other toppings like jalapeños and sour cream.) Eat straight from the bag, preferably with a spork.

★ ★ ★

TEXAS CAVIAR

On New Year's Day superstitious Texans take out a symbolic insurance policy by helping themselves to a heap of black-eyed peas—a practice that, according to tradition, guarantees one lucky day for each pea consumed. No one knows for certain how this ritual started, but one theory is rooted in horticulture: When planted, the legume replenishes the nitrogen content of soil and improves growth conditions, and thus the pea can be held responsible for the fortune of bountiful crops. To ensure prosperity, many Southerners eat the cowpeas Hoppin' John-style—boiled with a ham hock and served over rice—but a thoroughly native way to get them down is to polish off a bowl of Texas caviar.

Helen Corbitt, who reigned as Neiman Marcus's head chef for seventeen years, invented the dish in 1940, when she was asked to write a menu using only Texas products. At a loss for an acceptable recipe starring the peas that she admittedly didn't like, she decided to pickle them in oil and vinegar with garlic and onions and unwittingly produced what would become one of her most well known creations (it was so popular that Neiman Marcus later canned and sold it in stores). Her original recipe is a bit bare-bones and perhaps preferred among purists, but modern variations of the dish—including the one I like to prepare on January 1—feature diced green bell peppers, jalapeños, tomatoes, and cilantro. Best of luck!

Yield: Makes 4 servings

    2 fifteen-ounce cans cooked black-eyed peas
    ¼ cup olive oil
    ¼ cup red wine vinegar or more, to taste
    1 garlic clove, minced
    ¼ cup finely diced red onion
    ¼ cup finely diced green bell pepper
    ½ a diced jalapeño (stemmed and seeded)
    ½ cup diced tomato

1 tablespoon rough-chopped cilantro
½ teaspoon salt
cracked or freshly ground black pepper

Drain liquid from the peas and rinse. Place peas in a bowl, add remaining ingredients, and mix thoroughly. Can be stored in a glass container in the refrigerator for up to two weeks.

★ ★ ★

BREAKFAST TACOS

In 2010, the *New York Times* published an article titled, "Tacos in the Morning?" Texans were probably as confused by this headline as New Yorkers, but less by the idea that eating breakfast tacos is a "trend" making its way to the Big Apple than by the notion that anyone would dare question the good sense of starting the day with eggs, bacon, and cheese tucked into a fresh-off-the-griddle tortilla.

Admittedly this wholly Tex-Mex dish only dates back three or so generations, and no one knows who started the practice. (The murky history of breakfast tacos is similar to the genesis of tacos in general, which, according to Jeffrey M. Pilcher, author of *Planet Taco: A Global History of Mexican Food*, were invented relatively recently by eighteenth-century Mexican silver miners.) "There wasn't one thing that launched the breakfast taco scene, but it was a culmination of different things—and different cultures. It's part Texan, part Mexican, 100-percent Tejano," says Mando Rayo, an El

Paso native and author of *Austin Breakfast Tacos*. "Part of the fascination with this dish is that it takes comfort food and serves it for breakfast, at 8 a.m. or noon or at night—whatever time breakfast is for you."

At its core, a breakfast taco is a simple assemblage of ingredients. "The anatomy of a breakfast taco is a tortilla folded around a filling and salsa," says Rayo. The filling should cater to your taste on any given morning, but the typical base is scrambled eggs and another item, like fried bacon (American breakfast influence), chorizo (Mexican breakfast influence), or refried beans (Rayo's personal favorite). The tortilla can be corn or flour (in Austin, the epicenter of the breakfast taco craze, people tend to choose flour, while South Texans often opt for corn), but no matter which you choose, make sure they're handmade (raw tortillas bought from the store do in a pinch). And don't buy pre-packaged salsa if you can help it—because if it turns out to be made in New York City, well, true Texans know that's when you "get a rope."

HOMEMADE FLOUR TORTILLAS:

3 cups all-purpose flour
1 teaspoon salt
1½ teaspoons baking powder
4 to 5 tablespoons lard or shortening
¾ cup warm water

Mix dry ingredients in the bowl of a stand mixer. Cut in the lard with a fork or with your fingers until the fat is incorporated into the flour mixture.

Using the mixer's dough hook, slowly add the water to

the dry ingredients, kneading for 5 to 8 minutes, or until the mass is slightly smooth. Let rest for 15 or 20 minutes.

Portion the dough into a dozen or so 1-inch balls. Let those rest for another 15 to 20 minutes (this allows the gluten to relax so the tortillas are easier to roll out). On a lightly floured surface, working from front to back, flatten the dough ball with a rolling pin. Rotate the tortilla a quarter turn, and repeat the process until it measures roughly 7 to 8 inches in diameter.

Heat a *comal*, a flat griddle, over medium-high heat. Toast the tortilla on each side for roughly 45 seconds, or until each side is lightly browned.

MY VARIATION ON THE FAMOUS GREEN SAUCE MADE AT NINFA'S IN HOUSTON:

4 tomatillos, stripped of their leaves and washed
2 jalapeños
3 small garlic cloves
2 large avocados
½ cup tomato salsa
4 sprigs cilantro, leaves only
1 teaspoon salt
1½ cups sour cream

Heat oven to 350 degrees. Roast tomatillos, jalapeños, and garlic in shallow dish until the skin of the veggies blister. Puree the cooled ingredients in a food processor.

Halve the avocados, discard the pit, and spoon out the meat. Add the avocado, cilantro, salsa, and salt to the food processor. Pulse until smooth, and then transfer to a bowl. Stir in the sour cream. Cover with plastic wrap and refrigerate until ready to serve.

★ ★ ★

BARBACOA

When I was growing up, my father would buy barbacoa from the local *carnicería* on Sunday mornings. This delicacy, most typically served at weekend breakfasts (but certainly delicious on any day of the week and any time of the day) wasn't the "barbacoa" served by the likes of Chipotle; rather, this was *real* barbacoa: beef cheeks, or *cachete*, a collagen-loaded cut that is slow-roasted, a technique to enhance its savory flavor and silky texture.

These days, nearly all meat called barbacoa is either a baked or steamed rump roast, but historically people cooked a cow's head *en pozo*, in an underground pit. Armando Vera, the owner of Vera's Backyard Bar-B-Que in Brownsville, runs one of the last restaurants in the state that remains true to that centuries-old tradition. (Most cities have banned the practice, but his fifty-five-year-old establishment operates under a grandfather clause.) Vera's pit, which sells up to sixty-five heads a weekend, measures 3.5 feet wide, 5.5 feet long, and 5.5 feet deep and is lined with firebrick.

The first time I made my own authentic barbacoa, I enlisted the help of my friend Jason, who graciously offered use of the brick-lined pit dug out in his backyard. Not knowing where to buy an entire cow's head (would this be my inaugural trip to a local slaughterhouse?), I finally found a local butcher shop that sold the whole animal head. I stored the package in my fridge until the reckoning hour, occasionally curiously peeking into the box to behold what was then a novelty to me: an animal head chilling in my kitchen. (Being married to a butcher and avid hunter, I've seen quite a few more animal heads in the years since.) Part of me had wished I had asked them to trim out the cheek meat, a fine substitution for those who are a little more squeamish about making eye contact with their meal, but Jason assured me the final product would be worth it.

That evening, we set about preparing the meat.

EL PREPARACION:

Remove any trace of hide or hair, then rinse. Season liberally with salt and pepper. Traditionally, barbacoa pitmasters bundle the head in a burlap sack soaked with water, but we simply wrapped it tightly in a few layers of heavy-duty aluminum foil.

EL FUEGO:

Burn large chunks of wood—Vera prefers mesquite, which is plentiful in South Texas, though we used a combination of mesquite and live oak—for several hours, until the wood was reduced to glowing embers. We placed the meat in the pit, which Jason covered with a large piece of sheet metal to retain the heat. (The traditional method is to close off the pit with *maguey*, or agave, leaves.) Jason tended the fire for the next ten to twelve hours, replenishing the wood as necessary.

EL TACO:

The end result of this labor of love was roughly seven

pounds of smoked meat from the cow's head. Pull the meat from the bone and separate the *ojos* (eyes), *lengua* (tongue), and *mollejas* (sweetbreads) from the *cachete*, or combine a little of everything to make a taco *mixto*. Fill a corn tortilla with meat, onion, cilantro, and *un poquito de salsita. ¡Que sabroso!*

★ ★ ★

BRISKET

The sacred cow of Texas barbecue is brisket, but smoking one to perfection can be tough. So what's the secret? "Keep it simple," says Wayne Mueller, the third-generation owner of Louie Mueller Barbecue, in Taylor. "It's simple ingredients cooked with a simple process that simply requires patience and practice." Start with an untrimmed, or packer's cut, brisket that is well marbled and has at least a quarter-inch-thick fat cap. (When cooking, place the fat cap up so the juices are absorbed

into the meat.) Create a dry rub using one part salt and nine parts coarse-ground pepper, then liberally coat the meat with the seasoning and massage it in. Now you're ready to smoke a brisket that's a cut above.

THE WOOD:

Build your fire using regional hardwoods, such as mesquite in West Texas, hickory in East Texas, and post oak and pecan in Central Texas. "Never use conifers, like pine, because they emit a distasteful resin that permeates the food," Mueller says. When the coals glow red, the smoking can begin.

DIRECT HEAT:

Most backyard barbecuers use this method, but the brisket can quickly dry out because the meat sits directly over the coals. Avoid overcooking by soaking some wood chips in water (or in fruit juice for an extra layer of flavor) and adding them to the embers. The damp wood smolders and permeates the brisket with smoke. You can also offset the heat by raking the coals to opposite sides of the pit. Cook for 1½ to 2 hours per pound, at a temperature between 200 and 250 degrees, adding both dry and soaked wood chips as necessary to keep the temperature consistent.

INDIRECT HEAT:

This process, which employs an extension firebox on a smoker, produces fantastic barbecue but proves fickle even to practiced pitmasters; variables such as humidity and the size of the brisket can throw off results. "Rule number one is, open the pit as little as possible," Mueller says. The temperature should always stay the same (between 225 and 250 degrees) and heat escapes when you open the lid. Cook for 45 to 60 minutes per pound, until the internal meat temperature is at least 180 degrees. You can also use Mueller's feel test: "If you can poke your finger at least an inch deep into it, the brisket should be tender."

★ ★ ★

KING RANCH CHICKEN CASSEROLE

The sprawling King Ranch has inspired many things: myths and legends, books and movies, a line of Ford trucks and SUVs. But alas, the King Ranch chicken casserole did not spring forth from the ranch's cowboy kitchen. No one seems to know the exact provenance of this eponymous dish, but no respectable Junior League cookbook in the state would be complete without its own variant on the recipe.

A throwback to when dinner meant dumping half-of-a pantry-full of boxed and canned ingredients into a 9-by-13 pan and baking until the core temperature rivaled a caliche pad in West Texas, this layered dish is the Tex-Mex answer to lasagna. Tortillas replace pasta. In lieu of a laborious *ragú alla bolognese*, the filling is a mish-mash of humble Cheddar-Jack, simply seasoned chicken, and a straight-from-the-'60s amalgamation of "cream of" soups stewed with what I call Mexican *mirepoix* (onion, green bell pepper, and jalapeño). King Ranch casserole may not present well on the plate, but that gooey concoction and tortilla strata eats just fine.

Yield: Makes 10 to 12 servings

¼ cup canola or vegetable oil
1 white onion, chopped
2 green bell peppers, chopped
2 jalapenos, seeded, stemmed, and chopped
3 cloves garlic, minced
1 teaspoon chili powder
1 tablespoon salt
1 teaspoon cumin
1 teaspoon black pepper
1 can Ro-Tel tomatoes
1 can cream of mushroom soup
1 can cream of chicken soup
18 corn tortillas
1 cooked chicken, meat shredded
2 cups mixed Cheddar-Jack (shredded cheddar
 and Monterrey Jack cheeses)

Heat the oil in a large sauté pan over medium heat. Add the vegetables and sauté on medium-low about 5 minutes. Stir in the seasonings and cook for 1 minute. Add the Ro-Tel and the soups, and mix thoroughly and until heated through. Turn off heat and let mixture cool. Transfer to a large bowl, and incorporate shredded chicken. Add chicken stock if the mixture is too thick, and adjust seasonings to taste.

Preheat the oven to 350 degrees. Coat a 9-by-13-inch

baking dish with a thin layer of the chicken mixture. Line the bottom of the pan with six tortillas, making sure they overlap each other by about one third. Cover the tortillas with half the chicken mix. Sprinkle roughly a third of the cheese on top. Add a second layer of tortillas, the remaining chicken sauce, and another third of the cheese. Top with the remaining tortillas and cheese.

Bake for about an hour, until bubbling and lightly browned on top. Remove from the oven and let sit for roughly fifteen minutes, to allow casserole to set.

★ ★ ★

FRIED CHICKEN

Fried chicken is most frequently associated with the true South, but even if Texas doesn't necessarily count itself a constituent of that region, we heartily adopt its love of poultry that is dredged in milk and flour, before taking a swim in a vat of shimmery shortening. Plus, we dare someone from one of those states to top our favorite apocryphal story featuring the fried bird.

According to local lore, in 1883 Buffalo Gap and Abilene were vying to be named Taylor County's seat, a game-changing designation that would have economic implications for years to come. After a close election, the tie-breaking vote was cast by Judge John Watts Murray, a resident of Buffalo Gap. He voted in Abilene's favor. "Oral history indicates the citizens were upset," Heather Reed, Buffalo Gap Historic Village site manager, told the *Abilene Reporter-News* in 2014. "They went to the judge's house to voice their frustration and only found his chickens." As the story goes, upon finding those chickens, the irate community did to their necks what they had hoped to do to Judge Murray's, and, to the victors, such as they were, went the spoils.

While it's a bit of a grim tale, it's one that lives on in West Texas, where Perini Ranch, the famous steakhouse in Buffalo Gap, honors the somewhat dishonorable act by serving a special Sunday supper of "the Judge's Fried Chicken."

Yield: Makes 2 to 3 servings

1 whole chicken, parted
1 quart buttermilk
5 cups flour
2 teaspoons cayenne
2 teaspoons smoked paprika
2 teaspoons pepper
2 tablespoons salt
Shortening for frying

Place the cut chicken parts in a bowl or heavy-duty Ziploc

bag, and pour the buttermilk over the poultry to coat. Let it marinate for at least six hours (overnight is best).

When you're ready to cook the chicken, remove it from the refrigerator and let it sit at room temperature for 30 minutes. Meanwhile, mix the dry ingredients together on a plate. Set aside.

Heat 1½ to 2 inches of oil in a deep cast-iron skillet over medium-high heat until a thermometer reaches 350 degrees. (Lower the heat slightly, if necessary, to keep the oil from getting hotter.)

When the oil is ready and the chill is off the chicken, coat each buttermilk-drenched piece in the flour mixture and fry about twenty minutes, or until golden brown, flipping halfway through. (Poultry should temp at about 160 degrees at the thickest part of the meat.) Remove from the oil, place on a wire rack, and keep finished chicken in a 200-degree oven until all of the pieces are cooked.

★ ★ ★

KOLACHES

The one bright spot on the notorious stretch of I-35 between Dallas and Austin comes around the halfway point, at exit 353, the pull-off for West, Texas (often called "West comma Texas" by locals). This is one of the epicenters of Texas Czech culture, best known for its bakeries that sell kolaches, a pillowy pastry filled with sweet or savory concoctions. While the town is fortunate enough to have numerous sweet shops, the Czech

Stop, a gas station-bakery hybrid on the east side of I-35, arguably draws the most passersby. And arguably sells the most of these delicacies; according to one published estimate, they sell upwards of 24,000 dozen kolaches per month.

The sheer magnitude of volume certainly astounds, but as any amateur baker who's attempted to make kolaches can tell you, it's that much more impressive when you realize the patience and flour-coated fortitude it takes to make the damn things. Think it can't be that hard? Then know this: there's an old Czech saying that serves as a sort of warning to anyone audacious enough to undertake the difficult process of making kolaches: *Bez práce nejsou kolače.* Translation: "Without work, there are no kolaches."

Yield: 3–4 dozen kolaches, depending on size.

THE DOUGH:

2 packages dry yeast
¼ cup lukewarm water
1 teaspoon sugar
¾ cup shortening or margarine
¾ cup sugar
2 egg yolks
2 teaspoons salt
1 large can evaporated milk plus hot water to equal
   2 cups milk
6 cups flour (measure by lightly spooning into cup
   and leveling off)
melted butter for brushing

Dissolve yeast in water and sprinkle with 1 teaspoon sugar. In large bowl or mixer, cream sugar and shortening or margarine together. Add yolks and salt and mix well. Add the dissolved yeast and about a cup of the flour. Mix slowly with mixer. Add all the milk and continue adding the remaining flour, using mixer or stirring with a wooden spoon until dough becomes glossy. Cover; let rise in a warm place until double in bulk, about one hour.

After the dough has risen, cut off small portions of egg-size dough and shape into balls with a tablespoon. Place on a greased pan about 1 inch apart. Brush with melted butter, cover loosely and let rise until light.

Make a small indentation in each piece and place filling (recipe below) there. Sprinkle with topping (recipe below) and bake in a preheated 425-degree oven for 15 minutes. Brush the kolaches with melted butter when they come out of the oven and cool on wire racks. Kolaches are best the day they are made.

THE TOPPING (POSYPKA):

1 cup sugar
½ cup flour
¾ to 1 teaspoon cinnamon
2 tablespoons melted butter

Mix together until it resembles coarse meal. Store in the refrigerator.

APRICOT FILLING:

Cook a 10-oz package of dried apricots slowly in enough water to cover until fruit is soft and water is gone. Do not cover or fruit turns dark. Add 1½ cups sugar or more to taste and mash with a potato masher until well blended. This makes filling for about 2 dozen kolaches.

(This is Mrs. Jerabek's recipe which has been published many times in West's local newspaper.)

★ ★ ★

PECAN PIE

In Texas, a Thanksgiving spread without pecan pie is like Willie without Trigger. "People just expect it," says Bud "the Pieman" Royer, whose restaurant, Royers Round Top Cafe, in Round Top, ships thousands of pies across the nation during the holidays. "It brings back memories of Grandma baking pecan pie in her kitchen."

But more important than nostalgia, serving the dessert is a matter of Texas pride—the pecan is, after all,

our state tree. After you pick and shell your pecans, whip up this variation of pecan pie filling by one of Royer's favorites, a recipe by Ann Criswell, a former *Houston Chronicle* food editor and author of *Texas the Beautiful Cookbook*. "We like her recipe because she doesn't use dark syrup, which means it doesn't have that heavy molasses taste," he says.

THE DOUGH:

2½ cups flour
1 teaspoon salt
2 tablespoons sugar
12 tablespoons cold unsalted butter, cut into small chunks
½ cup chilled solid vegetable shortening, cut into small chunks
¼ cup bourbon, poured over three or four cubes of ice until it melts to make a bit less than ½ cup of liquid or 6 to 8 tablespoons ice water

THE FILLING:

5 tablespoons butter
1 cup brown sugar
¾ cup light corn syrup
3 eggs
1 teaspoon salt
2 tablespoons vanilla extract
2 cups pecan halves
1 tablespoon bourbon (optional)

PREPARING THE CRUST:

In a food processor, lightly pulse together 1½ cups of flour, sugar, and salt. Add shortening and butter, and pulse ten or fifteen times, until the mixture clumps together. Tump in remaining flour, and pulse additional six or eight times.

Transfer the crumbly flour mixture to a medium bowl, and begin adding the strained bourbon liquid or ice water. Gently mix into the dough with a spatula or wooden spoon. When the dough is slightly tacky, it's wet enough. Split into two portions, and wrap in plastic wrap. Refrigerate for at least an hour. (This recipe makes two 10-inch crusts; the other can be frozen for later use.)

Clear some counter space and lightly dust the surface, a rolling pin, the dough, and your hands with flour. Applying even pressure, roll out the dough with a back-and-forth motion. Give it a half turn, and repeat the process until it's roughly ⅛ inch thick. Dust the dough, and fold it in half twice, so it forms a wedge. Place the crust in a 10-inch pie pan, and unfold it.

Some people crimp the crust using fork tines, but Royer simply pinches the dough between his fingers. "This is homemade, which means it doesn't have to be perfect," he says. "Life's too short to make decorative leaves out of dough."

Blind bake the dough for a crispy, flaky crust. Pre-heat the oven to 425 degrees. Line the pie with parchment or foil, place pie weights or roughly one pound of dried beans on top, then bake for 12 to 15 minutes. Pull the pie from the oven, remove the pie weights and lining, then bake for 5 more minutes. Remove from the oven, turn the temperature down to 350 degrees, and pour the prepared filling into the parbaked piecrust.

PREPARING THE FILLING:

Melt the butter, and combine it with the sugar, corn syrup, eggs, salt, and vanilla. Pour the mixture into the pie shell. Place the pecan halves on top. ("It's important to use the halves," says Royer. "They taste better than the pieces.") Bake at 350 degrees for 45 to 60 minutes. It's ready when you stick a knife into the pie and it comes out clean.

★ ★ ★

MARGARITA

Few drink recipes have been as frequently adulterated and abused as the margarita. Bartenders looking to "put a new twist on an old classic"—mixologist parlance for "fix something that ain't broke"—too often apply a heavy hand of some saccharine-sweet sugary additive or a needless ornament like jalapeno slices or raspberry chunks (is this an appetizer or a drink?!). They may get an A for innovation, but more often than not, these variations end up ruining a concoction so simple and easy to mix that it all but ensures that even the drunkest among us can't muck it up—no matter how bad it might muck you up.

Yield: Makes one drink

    2 ounces silver tequila
    1 ounce Cointreau
    1 ounce juice from Mexican limes

With a lime wedge, moisten the rim of a tumbler. Put salt on a plate, then coat the rim. Fill a shaker with the

tequila, Cointreau, and lime juice. Shake well. Pour the mixture into the salted glass filled with ice, garnish with a lime wedge, and enjoy! (Alternate method for a straight-up margarita: swap the tumbler for a martini glass, add ice to the shaker with the liquids, then shake and strain into the glass.)

★ ★ ★

FURTHER READING

Franklin, Aaron, and McKay, Jordan. *Franklin Barbecue: A Meat-Smoking Manifesto*. Berkeley, CA: Ten Speed Press, 2015.

Perini, Tom. *Texas Cowboy Cooking*. Alexandria, VA: Time Life Books, 2000.

Walsh, Robb. *The Tex-Mex Cookbook*. New York: Broadway Books, 2004.

7

Relax Like a TEXAN

I think Texans have more
fun than the rest of the world.

Tommy Tune, actor, choreographer,
and Wichita Falls native

Allwork and no play make one a dull Texan. And we take—and make—fun any way we can get it.

Many of our good times revolve around sports. Our love for—some might say, obsession with—Friday night football is well documented. This passion is not unreasonable. To watch a well-coached team play high school football is to witness young people existing in that small sliver of life where determination and grit meets flair and finesse. Simply said, a talented Texas high school football team is a small marvel of humanity.

It also helps that our kids are damn good at the sport: roughly one-quarter of the NFL starting quarterbacks in 2014 call Texas home, and who doesn't want the chance to say they saw a hotshot pro play before he was famous?

But it's about more than the game. In small-town Texas, local high school sports draw big crowds because, well, there really ain't much more to do. That first weekend of the fall semester marks the welcome death to the boring, long, hot dog days of summer. For the fans sitting on those searing metal stadium bleachers in September, that inaugural blast of the kick-off whistle means cheering ferociously for your Lovelady Lions or Haskell Indians or Andrews Mustangs. When that season ends, fans pack into small school gymnasiums to rhythmically swivel their heads from side to side, watching basketball players move up and down the court as sneakers squeak across the floor. When the weather warms up, it's time for double plays and stolen bases on the baseball and softball fields; or to watch student athletes defy gravity in the high jump or spring down the track in dashes and relays. It's a flurry of activity that mothers, fathers, grandmas, grandpas, and proud aunts and uncles set their calendars by, politely turning down invitations from other friends and family by saying, "I can't that weekend; it's Homecoming."

That same Friday night fan-sanity certainly extends to our big city schools—the 6A programs based in the suburbs of Dallas and Houston produce some of the finest football players in Texas and the nation—but in the larger metro areas, our football fanaticism often centers on college and pro teams. From the Houston Texans (an unimaginative name, to be sure) evoking cheers (and jeers) in the Bayou City, to the Dallas Cowboys capturing the spirit of pretty much the rest of the state (and the nation—they are America's team, after all). Austin roots for the Longhorns like they're a pro team (and with all the money they have, they may as well be). As rich as "t.u." is in dollars, the Aggies are perhaps richer in tradition, with College Station being home to the "12th Man" and innumerable other rituals, as described in chapter 1.

We also dominate on the court. The Houston Rockets' back-to-back championships in the mid-nineties inspired Houstonians to call their hometown Clutch City. The Dallas Mavericks clinched the 2011 NBA Finals, defeating a much-ballyhooed (and equally much-reviled) Miami Heat. And all of South Texas lays claim to the San Antonio Spurs, who have won five championships under the Tim Duncan/Gregg Popovich-era, making that roster arguably one of the best in all of NBA history.

Baseball, too, is held dear in our hearts. A mere utterance of the name Nolan Ryan alongside the term "charging the mound" brings a smile to every Texan's face, whether she be a Rangers or an Astros fan, as The Ryan Express played for both. We also lay claim to another baseball institution: the Astrodome, the now-closed shrine once known as the "Eighth Wonder of the World."

Ask a Texan about our total dominance in sports, and we could go on and on (did I mention the Dallas Stars won a Stanley Cup, the Houston Dynamo were MLS Cup champions, and Austinite Ben Crenshaw won the coveted green jacket at the Masters?), but there's more to our leisurely lives. We hunt and fish (see chapter 5). We deep-fry, well, everything, and smoke the rest (see chapter 6). We polish the floors of honky-tonks and dance halls by scooting our leather boots across the long-leaf pine. (Since we are bragging a bit, you could say we excel at dancing: Patrick Swayze and Tommy Tune, two of the best hoofers America has produced, were both born in Texas.) We also completely invent games, like our state game 42, a variation on Bridge played with dominoes. And if all else fails, we get really creative (see the Luling Watermelon Thump, which hosts an event heavily focused on the spitting of Black Diamond watermelon seeds).

So while our pursuit of leisurely happiness is not too different than anyone else in America, we have perfected—or improved upon—a few manners of celebrating special occasions and filling free time.

★ ★ ★

SPIT WATERMELON SEEDS

Emily Post may have deplored any sort of public spitting as "disgusting" and "too nauseating to comment on," but such notions of etiquette have never stuck with the patrons of Luling's annual Watermelon Thump. Every June, the World Championship Seed Spitting Contest draws hundreds of spectators who hope to witness a Guinness-worthy spit (Luling resident Lee Wheelis set the record in 1989 at 68 feet 9⅛ inches). "There's not an exact science to it," says Jamie Nickells, the competition's chairman and the secretary-treasurer of the Thump Association. "But there are a few rules." Stated simply, they are as follows: (1) ammo must be harvested from the official Black Diamond melon, which is split on the premises; (2) each participant gets two chances on the "spitway," a 75- by 15-foot painted strip; and (3) the seed spit farthest wins.

Ready

Select a large, heavy seed and moisten your mouth with a bit of watermelon flesh. Center the seed on your tongue, with the tapered end positioned forward for better aim. If you're able, roll your tongue to make a barrel for your black bullet.

Aim

Approach the spitway, toes to the line, and inhale deeply *through the nose* (no one wants to perform the Heimlich maneuver). Lean back to achieve maximum force for propelling the seed.

Fire

Determine your technique: Champions either shoot up to create an arc and hope that a wind gust carries the seed or shoot down so it skips like a flat stone over still water (the bounce counts toward total distance). Abandoning all decorum, quickly expel your gathered breath through your rolled tongue. "Relax," says Nickells. "You're going to look silly, so get over it."

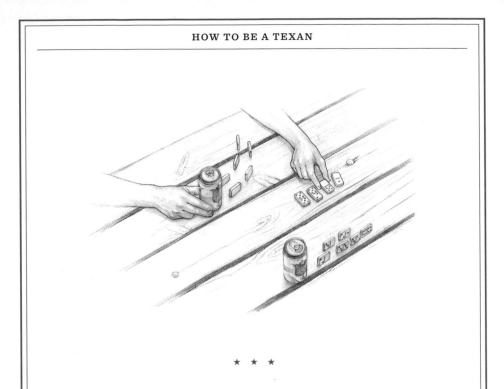

★ ★ ★

PLAY 42

About 120 years ago, two boys from Trapp Spring (now Garner) were caught in a forbidden pastime: playing cards. Their parents burned the offending deck and whipped the disobedient youngsters, but this led William Thomas and Walter Earl to find a loophole in the rules. "In those days Baptists considered card-playing to be the devil's work," says Dennis Roberson, the Fort Worth author of *Winning 42: Strategy & Lore of the National Game of Texas*. "But dominoes, for some reason, weren't sinful." So the enterprising boys replaced the cards with dominoes, invented a new game similar in style to bridge and spades, and dubbed it 42. Soon the game had scooted across Texas like an unhampered tumbleweed.

How to Play

Number of players: Four
Domino set required: Double-six
Setup: Players split into teams of two, with partners seated across from each other. After the dominoes are shuffled facedown, players draw seven tiles each to make up their hand (whoever shuffles picks last).
Objective: To be the first team to score seven marks by bidding and winning tricks or by setting your opponent.

Lingo Lessons

Winning what? Setting who? Above all, 42 is a bidding game, and your first order of business is to win tricks. A trick consists of the four dominoes played by each person at the table during a turn; the highest domino or the highest "trump" (more on trumps in a sec) played wins the trick.

There are seven tricks in a hand, and each trick is worth one point. Within these tricks, dominoes whose face value adds up to a multiple of five are also worth points. These dominoes—0-5, 1-4, and 2-3 (worth five points each), and 6-4 and 5-5 (each worth ten)—are known as "count."

When a player wins a trick that has count dominoes in it, his team is awarded one point for the trick plus the sum of the count. So for example, if you take a trick with 6-4 in it, that trick is worth eleven points: one point for the trick plus ten points for the count.

The game's name reflects the sum of all the points in a hand: 7 tricks + 35 total count = 42.

Strictly Bidness

There are variations on the game (like Nel-O or Sevens), but these adulterations are generally dismissed by dyed-in-the-wool players, so stick with the following basics.

After drawing your seven dominoes, each person must either bid or pass. When you bid, you're telling the table how many points you think your team can win; bidding must start at thirty points, and it can go all the way up to four marks (that is a dangerous gamble, but if it works, you're more than halfway to total victory).

Pass if you have a lousy hand; otherwise, you must always raise the previous bid. If everyone passes, the last person—that is, the person who shuffled—draws the short straw and must take a thirty bid. If it sounds like a raw deal, "Remember, you aren't just bidding your hand; you're bidding yours and your partner's," advises Roberson. (But no table talk allowed! Just hope and pray your partner can help you make your bid.)

The person who wins the bid gets to decide which suit of dominoes will be trump for the game (blanks, aces, deuces, treys, fours, fives, or sixes) and kicks off the first trick by playing a tile of his choice ("throwing a bone," in domino parlance).

Game On

Each player must then follow suit. The suit is automatically the higher number on the domino's face, unless it's a trump domino. If you can't follow suit, you may play any tile. The highest domino of a suit wins the trick, and a double is always highest in its suit. That is, unless a trump is played—in which case the highest trump wins. The winner of a trick then leads the next turn. After all seven tricks are played, the hand is over and the two teams tally their points. If the highest bidder makes his bid, his team gets a "mark" (similar to winning a "game" when you're playing a tennis match). If, however, he is "set" (fails to reach his bid), the opposing team gets the mark. The first team to score seven marks wins.

★ ★ ★

FLOAT THE RIVER

Some things never change, like the irrepressible desire to float a Hill Country river on a 100-degree day with, most naturally, a cooler of beer. And while the basic art of loading one's booze boat also remains the same no matter which river you choose (use a separate inner tube with a bottom, pump it with extra air for a snug fit around the cooler, be sure the cooler's top is secured so you don't wind up bobbing for brewskis), depending on where you float, there are a few rules to follow.

If you opt to tube the Comal or Guadalupe Rivers, be sure you first educate yourself on the City of New Braunfels's most recent rules (if you tube through one of the various outfitters along the banks, they'll give you the low-down too). These laws are vigorously enforced at entry points and exits and at random checkpoints along the banks, and for good reason: with more than 600,000 river rats descending on the area each summer to drink for long spells in the zapping heat, rowdy behavior is sure to follow. Be mindful and respectful of the rules—both formal and unwritten—or you might wind up being one of the more than two hundred people who receive tickets during particularly busy weekends.

Pack It In, Pack It Out

Everyone knows our state's fine anti-littering motto, but it's not just a good idea: it could save you up to $500, the max fine for leaving trash on or in the river. Tubing outfitters generally provide mesh bags to tie to your tube, but a trash bag poked with a few small holes (for less drag on your tube) will work in a pinch. Also, leave your electronics behind. You can Instagram another time.

Know How to Handle Your Booze

Many, but not all, local regulations permit alcoholic beverages, with some stipulations: (1) no glass, so leave behind the Lone Star longnecks and that jar of martini olives, (2) no containers under five fluid ounces (read: Jell-O shots discouraged), and (3) no "volume drinking devices," the formal term for beer bongs. But don't forget the koozies. Beer gets warm in a hurry, even in the cool waters of the Comal.

Your Rock Is Your Anchor

Bring a rope and designate a responsible party to secure the cooler vessel by tying it to himself or herself. (Note: Another rule is that there are no more than two tubes to a single person and flotation devices must be less than five feet in diameter at the narrowest point.) This beer ferry fairy should be able to navigate rapids while dragging extra cargo, have a good arm for tossing, and most important, not Bogart the booze.

The Cooler

One of the biggest changes from the "good ol' days," such as those always are, is no family-sized ice chests. Each tuber may bring one sixteen-quart cooler, which in turn must have a locking mechanism, i.e., a latch or a zipper. And forget the Styrofoam. The law also forbids all polystyrene carriers and containers.

★ ★ ★

TAILGATE

Around these parts, when September rolls around, it's the season to abandon reason and spend all your dough on football tickets for your favorite team. But as with all good times in Texas, the pre-party starts in the parking lot. To, ahem, kick off a tailgate celebration that everyone will want season passes to, it's all about creating an inviting atmosphere. First, adorn yourself in all that team paraphernalia you've bought over the years (jerseys, ball caps, cowboy boots in your team's colors, oversized foam finger), but distinguish yourself from a couch potato with shows of true commitment: face decals, dye jobs, strategic shaving, and, of course, body paint. Also imperative are your ride's trimmings (bumper stickers, hitch covers, specialty plates, insignia air fresheners, a fight-song horn) and any item with special powers (lucky boxers, that magical mustard-encrusted hot dog from last year). Now that the decorations are ready, it's time to stake a spot.

The Territory

More than fifty million tailgaters flock to stadium parking lots every year, so beat the crowds by arriving about four hours before game time, advises Stephen Linn, the former vice president of the San Antonio-based American Tailgater Association and author of nine tailgating books. Rules for position jockeying (arrival times, reserved areas) vary by venue, so call ahead or consult a guide. Coveted parking is near a grassy patch (for ample seating and spillover partying), but if you're in concrete country, find the end of a row and throw down some artificial turf for the same effect (just don't block traffic). Stake your claim with a tent, lawn chairs, and a portable landmark, like a blimp, for friends to find you.

The Nourishment

Beer? Check. Grill? Check. Propane? Oh, no. "The number one tip for good tailgating is to use a checklist," says Linn. Frequently forgotten necessities? Salt and pepper, a corkscrew, cutting boards, trash bags, and ice. Prep as much as you can the night before ("The point is to have fun with friends, not chop onions," Linn rightly points out) so that, come game day, you can focus on the essentials: your beer, your famous ribs, your next beer. The grill will always draw a crowd, but creating three stations—bar, dining area, kitchen—can help distribute the hovering hordes. Amid this controlled chaos, food safety is paramount: At the very least, pack a separate cooler and a set of knives for the raw meat. Salmonella is the ultimate buzz kill.

The Entertainment

Cold Shiner, close friends, and the anticipation of the day's matchup always equal good action *off* the field. Hard-core fans plug in plasma TVs and hook up satellite dishes to watch other games (you might add "generator" to that checklist). Lack those luxuries? There's no shame in listening to pre-game commentary on the radio—or bribing your neighbor with a juicy brat for a glimpse at his seventy-inch screen (lifelong friendships have been built on less). Rowdy tailgaters participate in such feats of skill and liver fortitude as flip cup (a relay-based drinking game) or beer pong (table tennis with alcohol). Gotta work the next day? Toss around the pigskin, start a pickup match of touch football, or be your own bookie in a friendly betting pool. Oh, yeah, and don't forget to go to the game.

★ ★ ★

TWO-STEP

Watching couples coast around at the honky-tonk may intimidate those with two left feet, but if a cowboy can dance, how tough is it, really? "Two-stepping is just walking to a beat," says Austin-based Rowdy DuFrene, a two-time United Country Western Dance Council World Champion. "While many variations exist, the true version follows a quick-quick-slow-slow pattern danced over six beats to music with four-four time."

To start, get into the traditional closed position. Leader, place your right hand on your partner's left shoulder blade and hold your left arm out to the side, slightly bent. Follower, lay your left arm on top of your partner's right arm, gripping the bicep, and slip your right hand into your partner's left. Crank up your favorite country crooner and get goin'.

1. *Quick*: On the first beat, leader, step forward with your left foot as your partner steps back with the right foot. Don't look down; lead with confidence to avoid bruising your partner's toes.
2. *Quick*: On the second beat, step forward with your right foot as your partner steps back with the left foot. Glide each foot past the other; never stop to close them together. Your mantra: "This is just like walking."
3. *Slow*: On the third beat, step forward with your left foot (sound familiar?) as your partner steps back with the right foot. Hold the fourth beat, with no movement; your partner mirrors you.

4. *Slow*: Complete the pattern by stepping forward on the fifth beat with your right foot as your partner moves back on the left foot. Hold the sixth beat, then give your partner a twirl. You just completed a true two-step!

A Few Extra Dance Tips

- Do mind your posture. A strong frame improves the quality of your dance (though one can keep it informal by hooking a thumb through a back belt loop).
- Don't be a kangaroo. Two-stepping is all about looking smooth, so avoid bouncing as you move.
- Do know your role. Leaders set the pace and followers are along for the ride. To best read each other's body language, stand close.
- Don't dominate floor space. The line of dance moves counterclockwise; beginners should stick to the inner circle so that experts can skate by any stuttering steppers.

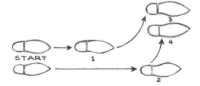

LEADER

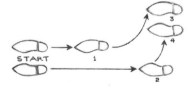

FOLLOWER

★ ★ ★

SQUARE DANCE

The square-dance social may seem like an antiquated notion, but dozens of clubs in Texas still preserve this pastime. "Square dancing persists because people enjoy the fellowship, the wholesome entertainment, and the exercise," says Wayne Morvent, who's been a caller for more than fifty years and works with the Bluebonnet Squares club, in Houston. "Also, we provide free cookies and coffee." But before you start to scoot across the floor, learn the most common movements, or dance steps, so you don't do-si-*d'oh*.

The Dress
Square dancers take pride in a polished look, so wear your best Western-style clothing. Gents traditionally opt for long-sleeved shirts (warm, yes, but they prevent other dancers from clasping a sweaty forearm), pressed jeans, and a bolo tie. Ladies customarily wear patterned dresses with petticoats or prairie skirts and simple jewelry (to avoid bruising their partner with a bulky bangle). For a little extra flair, some couples coordinate their outfits.

The Caller
Standing on a stage or off to the side, the caller is the director of the festivities. He counts off the band (or drops the record needle) and drives the dance by using two types of calls: a singing call (a structured, sixty-four-beat choreographed routine) and a patter call, which is

extemporaneous. Seasoned dancers sometimes prefer the patter because it's challenging and fast-paced. It may sound difficult, but experienced callers know how to keep it fun. "We want the dancers to dance," Morvent says, "not do geometric puzzles."

The Square

A square comprises four couples who move as a team, with multiple squares on the floor during a "tip," or dance session. When the music begins, the dancers follow the caller's movements. Some well-known ones are the promenade and circle-to-the-left, but there are a total of 68 mainstream movements. "It's like a game of Simon Says," Morvent says. Be prepared to raise your heart rate, as dancers complete as many as 128 steps per minute, but mind your manners by never exiting a square early (no matter how exhausted you are) and by applauding the caller at the end of a tip.

★ ★ ★

CUMBIA

Before waltzing into a Tejano nightclub—or into any big party in South Texas, for that matter—you should know how to dance cumbia. Originally a folk dance from Colombia, the cumbia shuffled across Latin America, picking up small changes along the way, and has comfortably settled here with a distinct Tejano flair. "The dance found at weddings and clubs in Texas isn't something you'll usually see in competition or that is formally taught," says Jessica Santiago, who has been grooving professionally for more than a decade and co-owns Calle Ocho, a studio in San Antonio. So where does one learn it? "By watching friends and family," she says. If your inner circle isn't hip to the steps, don't worry: The moves are wonderfully simple.

Crank up Selena's "Baila Esta Cumbia," stand with both feet together, and listen for the one-two-three beat. Then, on each beat:

1. Shift your right foot behind the left at an angle.
2. Take a small step in place with your left foot.
3. Move your right foot back to the starting position.
4. Repeat the sequence on the other side, starting with your left foot. (Your partner completes the steps on the opposite feet.)

See? Wonderfully easy.

Once you master these basics, add some hip bumps and a spin, and you'll soon look as though a practiced *prima* taught you everything you know.

★　★　★

FURTHER READING

Bissinger, H. G. *Friday Night Lights: A Town, a Team, and a Dream*. Boston: Da Capo Press, 1990.

Paredes, Américo. *Folklore and Culture on the Texas-Mexican Border*. Austin: University of Texas Press, 1993.

The WPA Guide to Texas. Texas Monthly Press, 1986. First published 1940 by Hastings House.

8

Tour Like a TEXAN

If you've ever driven across Texas, you know how different one area of the state can be from another. Take El Paso. It looks as much like Dallas as I look like Jack Nicklaus.

Lee Trevino, golfer and Dallas native

T o say Texas has it all is no exaggeration. The 98th meridian—that longitudinal line where, as famed Texas historian Walter Prescott Webb once wrote, "the woodlands of the east gave way to the arid plains of the west"—bisects our state. As a result, when it comes to natural beauty, we get a little bit of everything.

High up in the Panhandle, the Palo Duro Canyon, the second largest canyon in the country, cuts over 800 feet deep in certain parts of its 120-mile-long expanse. Behind the Pine Curtain are 23,500 square miles of forest, including pines, elms, mesquite, and ash trees, among others. The Gulf Coast (sometimes called the Third Coast) stretches for some 350 miles in Southeast Texas. Fourteen major rivers wind across the state; more than 11,000 streams wind across the land. Our thousands of square miles of blackland prairies make for enviably fertile farmland. It's a wonder it all fits in our boundaries, a marvel that once moved author Mary Lasswell to remark, "I am forced to conclude that God made Texas on his day off, for pure entertainment, just to prove that all that diversity could be crammed into one section of earth by a really top hand."

This statement could easily be extended to our wildlife. More than 5,000 flowering plants are native to Texas. Six-hundred-plus species of birds make their way through our airspace, a fact that makes Texas—specifically the coastal plains—one of the top birding destinations in America. Some twenty million Mexican free-tailed bats live in Bracken Cave, near San Antonio, a chittering congregation that makes it the largest population of bats in the world. (And the bats extend north to Austin, where the largest urban bat colony in North America hangs out under the Congress Avenue Bridge.) There are bighorn, bison, and bear; whales, dolphins, and otters; and, just to make things interesting, chomping alligators, stinging stingrays, and fifteen species of venomous snakes, among a host of other dangerous wildlife.

This embarrassment of natural riches inspires endless travelers to gobble up the sights and to cross items off of bucket lists (see that rare warbler in its habitat or visit that last national park in the far reaches of America, for example). Yet dotted along the way are innumerable other destinations, like world-class museums. The Nasher Sculpture Center in Dallas, a Renzo Piano–designed structure, houses a collection that includes works by Picasso, Matisse, and Miró. The Kimbell Art Museum in Fort Worth is a revered example of Louis Khan's exemplary architecture and boasts an expansion designed by Piano. And the Menil Collection in Houston is one of the most coveted private collections, a trove befitting metropolitan art meccas like Paris or New York. Even our small galleries are impressively curated, like the Panhandle-Plains Historical Museum in Canyon, the largest history museum in Texas.

Equally interesting are some of our quirkier spots. The Beer Can House in Houston was crafted by John Milkovisch with patience and love; 50,000 cans cover the siding and hang from the rafters like shimmering garlands. Tony Tasset, a Chicago-based artist, moved a giant eyeball sculpture to the Joule Hotel in downtown Dallas, a thirty-foot orb that watches you as you walk past. In 2005, European artists Elmgreen & Dragset installed *Prada Marfa*, a replica of the luxury fashion house's storefront plopped down in the middle of the desert and left it there in the stultifying heat, a sort of on-the-nose statement about consumerism and decay. Zipping north to Lubbock, the Buddy Holly Center decorated its front lawn with a five-foot-tall pair of the singer's famous black-rimmed glasses, and in the northeast corner of the state, in Paris (Texas, that is), the town nods to its French counterpart with a slightly smaller replica of the Eiffel Tower, topped with a red cowboy hat.

The list of must-see monuments could go on and on (don't forget the Fort Worth Stockyards! Guadalupe Mountains National Park, home to the state's highest point! The Texas State Cemetery in Austin! Galveston's flashy Pleasure Pier!), but there are a couple it would behoove the average Texan to visit.

★ ★ ★

THE TEXAS CAPITOL BUILDING

It must have been a particularly contentious time in the Texas Legislature when Houston legislator Bob Eckhardt called the Texas Capitol a place "built for giants but inhabited by pygmies." In the rooms and halls of this Italian Renaissance Revival-style building, our 181 legislators gather biennially to prove this adage wrong (or right) and debate, bicker, and—perhaps most often—barter with each other. Which makes it only fitting that the Capitol owes its existence to one of the most impressive bargains struck in Texas history. After a fire destroyed the state's third capitol in 1881, the Lege traded 3,000,000 acres in the Panhandle to contractors for the construction of a new building. (Those three million acres later became the XIT Ranch, the largest ranch under fence in the nation.)

The new Capitol opened April 21, 1888, a six-year-long project that saw various challenges, including a near-catastrophic architectural miscalculation of its defining dome and a labor boycott in protest of quarrying the hallmark "Sunset Red" pink granite used for the building's exterior. Yet despite some problems and setbacks (including another fire in the 1980s), the Capitol endures, standing grandly at 302 feet tall and distinguished as the largest (by square footage) of all state capitols; making it, in its own way, a giant among, well, you get the rest.

The Grounds

Situated where Congress Avenue T-bones 11th Street, the Capitol sits on one of Austin's highest points, a commanding presence enhanced by state-mandated "view corridors" that prohibit other structures from obstructing sight-lines of the building. Even from a distance, people typically first notice the Goddess of Liberty statue, an homage to Athena, the Greek goddess of wisdom; she's perched proudly on the pink dome at 15 feet, 7½-inches, clutching a sword in her right hand and thrusting a gilded star high in the air with her left.

South: Encircling most of the twenty-two-acre grounds is a historical iron fence, which has entry points at each major cardinal direction, but the south facade is by far the most famous and photographed. Stroll up the five hundred-foot-long "Great Walk," a black and white diamond-patterned stretch of pavement shaded by trees and lined with statues, stop to read the historical markers for the four oldest monuments: the Heroes of the Alamo, Volunteer Firemen, Confederate Soldiers, and Terry's Texas Rangers. (When reading signs for these and the fifteen other monuments on the grounds, always remember to take them in the context of their sometimes warty history.)

West: Continue along the sidewalk toward a depression in the land directly opposite the Capitol's west entrance. This grassy bowl was once a small man-made pond, a picturesque landscape that encouraged water-side picnics and political reflection—until summertime when it likely became a breeding ground for blood-hungry skeeters. They drained the pool in 1926.

North: As you continue rounding the grounds, stop to smell the Tyler roses (my personal favorite spot) and to take a picture with the forever-frolicking kids of the Tribute to Texas Children monument. You'll likely also notice the iron gate doesn't close the north end of the grounds, but there still is a barrier of sorts; granite gateposts remain from the original north section fence.

East: If all this walking has made you thirsty, hydrate at the ornate replication of a cast-iron drinking fountain that once pumped up water from an artesian well that some believed had magical properties. Step on the foot pedal for water (that now comes from a regulated water source), and be thankful the city didn't replicate the community metal drinking cup that hung from a chain on the original fountain.

The Interior
If the exterior of the Capitol borrows from Italian Renaissance design, the interior decorations have a much more distinctly—yet distinguished—Texan tilt. Look closely for the sometimes subtle or hidden details. (Also note there is a metal detector and security screening required for entrance.)

First floor: In the South foyer, pay respects to Sam Houston and Stephen F. Austin, the forefathers of Texas who are honored with life-sized marble statues carved by Elisabet Ney, the famous Austin sculptor. Continue on to the rotunda, where you must do the following, no matter how silly you think it sounds: 1) tilt your head back, 2) lock sight on the Texas star 218 feet above you, and 3) whirl around in a circle. Shake off the dizzies and regain equilibrium by slowly pacing the terrazzo floor inlaid with the seals of the six nations whose flags have flown over Texas: the United States, Mexico, France, Spain, the Confederacy, and the Republic of Texas. But don't say anything here you wouldn't want the governor to hear; the rotunda acts as a whispering gallery, amplifying sound.

Second floor: Walk up the east wing staircase (or take the elevators) to the Senate chambers, where the original walnut desks commissioned for our thirty-one senators are still in use, microphones tucked into the space that once housed ink wells. (Another fun detail: the bulbs in the light fixtures hanging from the ceiling spell "Texas.") While the portraits of numerous Texas leaders—Lorenzo de Zavala, Lyndon Baines Johnson, and Barbara Jordan, to name a few—are certainly worth admiration, an hour can easily pass examining the intricate and detailed oil paintings of our state's most famous battles: *Dawn at the Alamo* and *The Battle of San Jacinto.* Cross over to the west wing to the House chamber, the largest room in the Capitol, for a possible glimpse of the original 1836 San Jacinto Battle Flag, one of only two flags remaining from the revolution.

Third floor: While the third floor is primarily office space and the entries to the House and Senate galleries, there are plenty of marvels of craftsmanship, like the beautifully carved wood door frames that are secured with elaborate, custom-designed, eight-by-eight, seven-pound bronze hinges inscribed with the words "Texas Capitol."

Fourth floor: People who make it up to the fourth floor typically come to see the final set of governors' portraits (and with only five spots left to fill, and assuming Governor Greg Abbott and his successors each serve just a single term, the wall will run out of room for new guvs around 2039). But it's on the fourth floor that one of the Capitol's greatest hidden treasures can be seen. Well, sort of seen. The blue oculi, twenty-four panes of intricately patterned glass, were installed in the skylight structure behind the Texas flag on the north wing roof. They're nearly impossible to see from either the inside or outside, but during certain times in the day, streaks of bright blue light are cast on the walls of the atrium, one more little secret in a building that's all too full of them.

★ ★ ★

BARTON SPRINGS

On a cloudless, hot summer's day at Barton Springs Pool—a three-acre, spring-fed oasis nestled in the center of Austin's Zilker Park—it's easy to melt into the scene. Exposed flesh of all shades and bodies of all sizes can be seen, people lounging and milling around the pool's edges. Impossibly fit swimmers dodge people bobbing aimlessly in the water. The diving board thumps rhythmically as experts and novices alike jump and flip off its edge. Kids squeal and splash. Lifeguards bleat on whistles. Idle chatter thrums through the air.

But as the activity pulses, try to shut it all out and imagine the springs of a few lifetimes ago. To a time thousands of years ago, when it was a resource for Tonkawa and Lipan Apache tribes, Native Americans who believed the waters had healing powers. Even if you don't believe in such things, suspend your doubts momentarily and admit that it's hard to deny that there *is* something mystical about the pool. Sure, science can explain why, just below the diving board, more than thirty million gallons of fresh water pump out of Parthenia, the fourth-largest spring in Texas, which is named after the pool's namesake's daughter. And, there's a geothermic reason why the average temperature stays between 68 and 70 degrees year-round. But there's magic in a place where Taoist monks made it a mission to bless the waters. Where an endangered salamander evokes enough sympathy that the pool closes once a week to preserve its habitat, crowds and commerce be damned. Where the communal atmosphere flattens class, age, and other defining characteristics that shape human perceptions.

And just as there are many reasons to revere the springs, there are many ways to enjoy them.

For the Relaxers
The grassy knolls sandwiching the banks of the springs beckon swimmers to lay out a towel and lounge with a

book, but if you want the same experience in the water, floats are permitted in the deep end of the pool.

For the Fitness Fanatics

If you want to do laps and beat the crowds (and, during the summer, the entry fee), arrive before 8 a.m. Also, don't let the idea of chilly water prohibit winter swims; first off, the springs' temperature is a consistent 68 degrees year-round, which often makes it warmer in the water than outside during the coldest months. Plus cold water is said to improve circulation and immunity, be good for hair and skin cells, and relieve stress and depression.

For the Kids

The south end of the pool is relatively shallow, with lots of flat areas for wading with small toddlers. Just be careful: algae makes the rocks slick, so they should be navigated carefully.

For the Adventurous

Catch some air and leap off of the diving board near the deep end of the pool. Or, if you're feeling you might be after a different sort of titillation, wait until 9 p.m. and attend night swim, when free spirits take advantage of the free admission.

★ ★ ★

GRUENE HALL

When *Vogue Living Australia* named Gruene Hall one of the world's best bars, the defining criterion was that each place have "a sense of history and a commitment to another era of hospitality." Gruene Hall, a 6,000-square-foot building constructed in 1878, is the state's oldest continuously run dance hall, and has been a tour stop for big-ticket acts such as *sucks in breath* Ernest Tubb, Bo Diddley, Merle Haggard, Loretta Lynn, Jerry Lee Lewis, Little Richard, and Tanya Tucker as well as the launching pad for now-legendary singers such as Kris Kristofferson, Willie Nelson, Lyle Lovett, Townes Van Zandt, and George Strait. So, history? Check.

As for "a commitment to another era of hospitality," well, that's the defining criterion of a true Texas dance hall. For well over a century, these places served as community hubs, where entire families congregated to break bread, drink libations, and let their boots polish the pine during a polka. Unfortunately, much like homespun hospitality, Texas dance halls are vanishing; their numbers have gone from 1,000 in their prime to only a few hundred now.

The town of Gruene (pronounced "green") narrowly escaped a whispered end. During the Depression, nearly all the stores were shuttered. Luckily, the hall managed to stay open. Then in 1975, during the heyday of the Austin-centered Outlaw country movement, Pat Molak started looking to buy a nearby dance hall to feature all this great new talent budding in Texas. A tip from a friend led him to Gruene, where he bought the languishing hall, and the rest is internationally acclaimed history.

On any night of the week on any day of the year, the Shiner is cold, the license plate-patched floors creak under the weight of dancers, and a little breeze whistles through the windows screened with chicken wire. But there are many shades of Gruene, and depending on what you're in the mood for, you should plan your trip accordingly.

Hot in the Summer

Part of the appeal to Gruene Hall is that even the big shows feel relatively intimate. Acts like Robert Earl Keen, Hayes Carll, Jerry Jeff Walker, and Patty Griffin could easily draw thousands of fans, but the 800-capacity hall makes it seem like you're at a party with several hundred of your new good friends. But it'll still be snug. If you're not the kind of person who likes waiting in lines (for security or beer or the bathroom) the $20-plus bills might not be for you.

Reasons for Off-Season

If you ask a local about a visit to Gruene, they'll probably tell you that for the full experience, you should go on a Saturday night in the summer. Which is true, in a way. But they're also probably trying to keep it a bit of a secret that some of the best shows at the hall are on rainy winter weeknights. The shutters are pulled tight, the wood-burning stoves emanate cozy heat, and a reliably good band—quite possibly the next big country breakout—plays to a small crowd that knows how to dance.

★ ★ ★

CADILLAC RANCH

Road trips are the quintessential American pastime, a rite of passage for vacationing families who pack into a car to cram in as much sightseeing as possible. For years, Route 66—a stretch of highway from Chicago, Illinois to the Santa Monica Pier, in California—served as "the Mother Road" for these journeys, and tourist destinations flourished along the way. One such landmark juts out of the flat Panhandle plains, just a few miles west of Amarillo, a public art installation that is one of the most famous roadside attractions in America: *Cadillac Ranch*.

In 1974 an art collective from San Francisco called Ant Farm buried ten Cadillacs nose-first into a wheat field alongside Historic Route 66. (The project was funded

by legendary Amarillo businessman and philanthropist Stanley Marsh 3.) The models, ranging from 1949 to 1964, represented the latest versions of the car's famous tail fin. "To me, it was a dolphin idea," Ant Farm founder Doug Michels told *Texas Monthly* in 1994. "You know how the wheat waves and ripples in the wind? Well, suddenly we imagined a dolphin tail fin sticking up out of the wheat. Then the dolphin tail fin became a Cadillac tail fin. That was it. There was *Cadillac Ranch*." The whimsical pop art project quickly captured the nation's attention, and decades later—even after it was relocated two miles westward to avoid encroaching development—Cadillac Ranch remains "the hood ornament of Route 66" (though, technically, the road is now I-40).

Over the years, it has become a playground for graffiti artists, and the public is encouraged to make its mark. Decades-worth of paint has turned the cars' exteriors into a mottled crust, but the silhouette is as classic as ever.

Know Before You Go . . .

BYOP, or bring your own paint. If you're heading west from Amarillo, there's a Home Depot on the way.

The cars are buried on private land, but visitation is welcomed and encouraged. Park alongside the south side of the I-40 frontage road (there's plenty of room), and enter the pasture by walking through the unlocked gate. The cars are roughly seventy-five yards from the road, but you can't miss 'em; they're the ten Cadillacs buried in a field.

Be prepared for some grime and grit. This isn't a state-funded or oft-tended site. There will likely be litter and trash. (If you really wanted to earn some karmic brownie points or be a Good Samaritan, you could bring a Hefty bag and be a steward of the land.)

If you plan to spend some time on your art, remember that you're going to be working in an open Texan prairie. Wear a hat and some sunscreen.

The sun isn't the only natural element that could be an enemy. Try to avoid going after a heavy rain; the field gets muddy, which is a problem compounded by the heavy foot traffic by other tourists.

Second only to paint in importance is a camera. The whole point of making the trek is for the photo op. Before posing, get creative with some era-specific props, like cat-eye sunglasses, a glass-bottle Coke, or a Don Draper–inspired fedora.

★ ★ ★

DEALEY PLAZA

Invariably, when the topic of the assassination of President John F. Kennedy comes up, talk turns to conspiracy theories, like the infamous second shooter at the grassy knoll, Cuban involvement, or the ultimate mafia vendetta. As easy as it is to fall down the rabbit hole of some of these impressively documented theories, the Warren Commission's ten-month investigation into the matter concluded that Lee Harvey Oswald acted alone in the assassination of the thirty-fifth president. (They also found that Jack Ruby, the man who killed Oswald outside of the Dallas Police Headquarters, acted alone.)

As such, that is how history is presented at Dealey Plaza and the Sixth Floor Museum, located in the former Texas School Book Depository, from which Oswald fired the fatal shots at 12:30 p.m. on Friday, November 22, 1963. Regardless of what you might believe about the circumstances surrounding the tragedy, Dallas has long wrestled with how to confront the horror that happened in its downtown—an event that earned the city the unfortunate moniker "City of Hate"—while still honoring the legacy of one of America's most beloved presidents. The result is a smartly curated museum and the long-overdue renovation of Dealey Plaza, a three-acre park maintained by the City of Dallas. A trip through the public park gives an eerie, if fascinating, glimpse into one of our nation's greatest tragedies.

The Sixth Floor Museum
Located in what was the Texas School Book Depository (now the Dallas County Administration building), the museum inhabits the sixth floor, the same floor from which Oswald aimed his rifle. In 1972, the building was almost demolished (it was later sold to Dallas County, which now operates office space out of the first five floors). Roughly 350,000 people a year make the trek to the museum, which offers audio tours, radio recordings and television footage broadcast of the president's motorcade, and even Abraham Zapruder's film, which caught the incident on camera. Those hoping for a

macabre experience or to look through the window of the "sniper's nest" will be disappointed; the museum is tastefully appointed, and the window is glassed off.

Dealey Plaza

In 1993, the plaza was named a National Historic Landmark. This designation has kept the streets and surrounding buildings and structures from being drastically altered from how they looked in 1963. People familiar with the footage of the assassination will be taken aback by how unchanged the city is here, which makes it that much easier to transport yourself to the horrible moment in time. For even clearer visual guidance, there's an X on Elm Street to mark the exact spot where the president was shot.

The Grassy Knoll

On the northwest side of the plaza, the infamous grassy knoll continues to draw crowds. (When the eyewitnesses were interviewed, more than thirty people reported hearing shots from the area by the grassy knoll and the triple underpass.) The sloping patch of grass is now often populated by vocal conspiracists who sell literature questioning the official story of the assassination, evidence that no matter how many years pass, this tragedy continues to fascinate even those who weren't alive to bear witness.

* * *

SOUTHFORK RANCH

It's no "Houston, we have a problem," but the phrase "Who shot J. R.?" did almost as much to catapult a different Texas city onto the international stage. Undoubtedly the most famous whodunit in television's most famous cliffhanger, the third-season finale of *Dallas* captured the world's attention. More than ninety million viewers watched the episode that finally revealed the answer (no spoilers), and it remains the second-highest rated single television broadcast in US history (surpassed only by the *M*A*S*H* finale and not counting sports events), a feat that cemented *Dallas*'s legacy as a global phenomenon.

For fourteen seasons—357 episodes that aired from April 2, 1978, to May 3, 1991—an audience spanning ninety-six countries watched in more than fifty languages as the Ewing clan, an oil and ranching family, battled for power using blunt-force capitalism, tawdry sex schemes, and other epically sleazy tactics befitting a soap opera based in Texas. The stage for this melodrama is set in the beloved opening credits, with aerial shots

of bobbing pump jacks and roaming cattle juxtaposed against a modern city skyline and the shining Dallas Cowboy's stadium. But the minute-long montage culminates in a sweeping shot of Southfork, "the most famous White House west of DC." The two-story house, with its white fence and yellow awnings, became as famous a character as Jock and J. R. or Miss Ellie and Sue Ellen, even if it was primarily only used for exterior shots and a few interior shots during the show's first season.

The $5 million 340-acre ranch, which was founded as a horse farm in 1970, began admitting tourists in 1985, and while locals might sniff at the notion of a visit, Southfork symbolizes the brassiness of both the fictional and real Dallas.

Five Must-Snap Photo Ops

Channel your inner Patrick Duffy, a.k.a. Bobby Ewing, or Victoria Principal, a.k.a. Pam Ewing, and get in front of the camera for your close-up.

At the Ranch Entrance

The white arch framing the tree-lined road that leads to the mansion may not factor into the show as a main point of reference, but the proof you've been (even if you just stop on the side of the road to take a quick pic) is written right on the sign: Southfork Ranch proudly displayed in all caps.

In J. R. and Sue Ellen's Bedroom

The bedroom is an exact replica of the Hollywood set used for Sue Ellen and J. R.'s bedroom. You can sit on the bed the couple shared—sometimes icily—and admire the luxurious bathtub Sue Ellen would have soaked in with her glass of booze handy, or, if it's all too much, faint on the unapologetically '80s-patterned chaise lounge.

Next to Jock's Mark V
When it comes to cars in Texas, Jock Ewing's 1977 Lincoln Mark V holds nearly as much clout in Texas as the pink Mary Kay Cadillac (almost). The original vehicle—with a mere 25,000 miles on the odometer—is a symbol of Big Texas Rich (the *big* being especially pertinent here, as the car measures 19.3 feet long).

On the Second Floor Balcony (Pool in the Background)
After you put your feet in the famous pool that the Ewing family gathered around, Bobby in his speedo and the girls in their body-baring bikinis, hustle upstairs to take a photo from the balcony that J. R. and his son jumped from to escape a fire in the house.

With the Gun
While there's no replica of J. R.'s office for you to lie outside of to know what it was like to be the most famous near-murder victim in television history, the gun that shot J. R. is on display. As for his trademark ten-gallon Stetson? Larry Hagman, who played the despicable antihero, donated it to the Smithsonian National Museum of American History, which ain't a shabby place to hang a hat.

★ ★ ★

SPINDLETOP

A mere 375 days after the turn of the twentieth century, a momentous event hurriedly ushered in the modern era of Texas. Oilmen had spent weeks drilling to a depth more than 1,000 feet into Sour Springs Mound, a salt dome a few miles south of Beaumont, hoping to come into some "Texas Tea." And at about 10:30 in the morning on January 10, 1901, the teacup runneth over.

It started with a bit of a whimper; the ground began rumbling and the derrick rattled before producing a bang: a torrent of black gold erupted from the Lucas gusher, bursting 150 feet into the air. It spewed 100,000 barrels a day for nine straight days (nearly $30,000,000 worth of oil in today's dollars) before it could be tamed. By the time the well was capped, it was producing more oil per day than all of the other wells in America combined. The petroleum industry of Texas—and the notion that everything is bigger here—was born.

So was the boomtown. Within a year of discovering Spindletop, the oilfield was punctured with more holes than a cribbage board, roughly twenty wells per acre, becoming a dense forest of four hundred derricks by 1903. Money came in to Spindletop as fast as oil poured out, with some published accounts estimating that the field generated $50 million, what now amounts to over $1 billion. People were making money hand over fist . . . quite literally, in some cases. One man sold his land for $20,000; fifteen minutes after the close, the buyer unloaded the tract to another investor for $50,000. (The

town certainly earned its reputation as "Swindletop.")
Each day, hundreds of people moved to nearby Beaumont, streaming out of trains and swelling the town's
population from 10,000 to 50,000. Restaurants and
hotels cropped up, and, like weeds after a heavy rain, the
number of saloons increased at a breakneck clip, from
twenty-five in 1900 to eighty-one in 1903.

The notion of explosive growth fueled by oil has since
become almost a Texas stereotype, but the first cut is the
deepest. To commemorate the most famous gusher in
American history, the Spindletop-Gladys City Boomtown Museum built a replica of the boomtown, complete
with a post office, saloon, barbershop, blacksmith, drug
store, and mercantile store.

The town is the quaint Texas version of Colonial Wil-
liamsburg, and while occasionally the museum stages an
impressive re-enactment of the gusher (complete with a
150-foot jet of water shooting up out of the replica derrick), the real site of the gusher sits approximately one
mile south of Texas Highway 69, just west of Spur 93. It's
on private property, but the view from Spindletop Park's
elevated platform is a clear sight line to a flagpole that
marks the spot where history began.

★ ★ ★

MIRADOR DE LA FLOR

Few shadows in Texas music loom as large as that of Selena Quintanilla-Pérez, known mononymously as Selena. In her brief twenty-three years, the Queen of Tejano recorded five solo studio albums, scooped up thirty-six Tejano Music Awards, inked a deal with Capitol Records, and signed on to be a spokesperson with Coca-Cola. But her life was tragically cut short on March 31, 1995, when Yolanda Saldívar, the president of her fan club and manager of her clothing boutique, shot her outside of a Days Inn in Corpus Christi, her hometown. Yet Selena's legacy lives on. Decades after her death, her music is still on regular rotation on Tejano stations. Warner Bros. produced a slick biopic based on her life, starring Jennifer Lopez in the title role. And more than 30,000 visitors annually stream to Mirador de la Flor, the Overlook of the Flower, a memorial on Corpus Christi's Shoreline Boulevard, to honor the fallen star.

The overlook, one of nine *miradors*, or Spanish-style gazebos that line the bay-front and celebrate important moments in the city's history, was constructed and unveiled in 1997. Its defining feature is a five-foot-eight bronze statue of Selena sculpted by local artist H. W. "Buddy" Tatum. It's an appreciable likeness, right down to the outfit: she wears one of her signature bustiers, a studded jacket, pants, and cowboy boots as she loosely grips a microphone in her left hand. It also conveys Selena's reputation as a down-home and approachable rising star, depicting her leaning against a pillar, leg hitched up as she gazes out toward the bay.

Whether you're a fan or not—and you only would *not* be if you haven't heard her contagiously upbeat music—Selena remains one of the most talented musicians the state has ever produced, and, as such, deserves to be honored for her contributions to Tejano culture. Or, as a plaque at the statue best summarizes it, "Selena's stage is now silent, yet her persona enriched the lives of those she touched and her music lives on."

Know Before You Go . . .

The monument is a public space and requires no fee to see. However, the city added a four-foot stainless steel barrier around the statue in 2000 to protect against graffiti. When taking photos, don't hop the fencing and be mindful of the family's wishes that the monument be treated with respect.

To bring white roses. The flower was Selena's favorite, as evidenced by the nearby mosaic murals of white roses and the large white bloom affixed to the pillar next to the singer. Keeping fresh bouquets near the statue enlivens the atmosphere.

That it's okay to sign your name to one of the bricks around the monument. Inscriptions are written in English and Spanish, and some are just illustrated with images honoring the singer. But choose your words with care; this is a family-friendly monument, after all.

Parking is difficult to find, especially on the weekends.

For a little more context and history on Selena's life, visit the Selena Museum, roughly six miles inland from the memorial. Here, you can see her famous Astrodome costume, the dress she wore to the Grammys, and her lipstick-covered microphone.

★ ★ ★

THE ALAMO

"Remember the Alamo." This battle cry, known the world over, has made the historic site perhaps the most famous place in Texas. And while Texans have long revered the courage and tenacity of the 189 defenders who held the Alamo for thirteen days against General Antonio López de Santa Anna and his Mexican army, the battle—which was ultimately lost in the early hours of March 6, 1836—rose to the stuff legends are made of after the five-part television miniseries *Davy Crockett* aired in the 1950s and John Wayne's big-budget film *The Alamo* was released in 1960.

Of course, innumerable other books have been written, films made, and television shows aired depicting the events of that deadly day. Everyone is familiar with images of James "Jim" Bowie, with his menacing knife in hand, and William Barret Travis declaring "I shall never surrender or retreat" and extolling the virtues of "victory or death" before drawing a literal line in the sand. These tales of heroics enrapture America and help to keep the Alamo—one of five Spanish missions in San Antonio that are now designated UNESCO World Heritage sites—an international travel destination, now drawing more than 2.5 million people to the 4.2-acre complex annually.

But over the decades, its epic history has come under intense study. Facts have been questioned, motives of both sides scrutinized. Myths perpetuated by popular culture have further muddled what we collectively think we know occurred in 1836. As a result, some Texans absolutely loathe the Alamo and what it stands for, while others are able to appreciate it in its historical context.

No matter which side of history you stand on— whether you regard the defenders as heroes or villains— there's no denying the magnetic pull of the Alamo. The iconic shrine where many of them died—defined by its world-famous curved parapet, pockmarked walls, and surprisingly small size—remain as alluring and power- ful as ever.

Stand in the Spot Where . . .

The largest piece of the defenders' heavy artillery sat. An 18-pounder cannon kept the Mexican army at bay, and it is this cannon that Travis likely fired in response to Santa Anna's call for surrender.

William Barret Travis, the co-commander of the garrison, was killed. Travis was shot early in the final battle, killed while blasting his shotgun into the soldiers attempting to besiege the north wall. According to some reports, he fell about twenty feet from the post office's southwest corner, near what is now a stairwell leading to a nondescript side entrance. The north wall was eventually breached, and it was through this hole that Mexican soldiers entered the Alamo compound.

The Mexican army blasted open the doors of the barracks. One historian notes that the Cenotaph, a white marble statue designed by the Italian sculptor Pompeo Coppini as a monument to the fallen, roughly marks the spot where the cannon was wheeled.

Jim Bowie, who fell too ill to command, was bayoneted while laid out in a cot. Some dispute the exact location where Bowie died—either in the second story of the Long Barrack or in the church—but many believe the former, and there is a bronze marker at the old south gate that marks the site.

The most intense and bloodiest, hand-to-hand fighting occurred. Walk along the Long Barrack (the oldest building on site), where the Texians retreated after the walls were breached.

The women and children of the Alamo sought protection during the siege and battle. They hid in an interior room that was protected by three-foot-thick walls. After the men were killed, Mexican troops found the women and children, including Susannah Dickinson and her baby, Angelina, who lived to tell their tales. (One of her recollections is of the final words of her husband, Captain Almaron Dickinson: "Great God, Sue, they're in the walls.")

Davy Crockett is said to have fallen when he died. As with Bowie, there are conflicting accounts of whether Crockett was killed in battle or executed after the Mexican troops took the Alamo, but Dickinson later recounted that his body fell just outside the northwest corner of the chapel, now marked by a Mexican olive tree.

★ ★ ★

THE WINDOW TRAIL AT BIG BEND NATIONAL PARK

For people who have visited Big Bend National Park, it's astounding to learn that it's one of the least-visited National Parks in the system. Sure, it's far-flung—600 miles from Houston, 530 from Dallas, and even 290 miles from El Paso, the closest big city—and yes, on the drive out there, the flatness seems interminable. But when you're driving toward the park along a stretch of monotonous highway, mountains hazily come into view, a sight that, as it gets crisper, almost seems as though it must be a hallucination from all the Doritos, Corn Nuts, and beef jerky you've eaten on the road.

Once inside Big Bend's boundaries, it's easy to be transported to what feels like another era . . . or another planet. Encircled by panoramic vistas of mountains and desert, peaks stab into the limitless blue sky and stretches of sand peppered with spiny plants yawn for miles in all directions. As the sun sets in the west, light dances off of the volcanic rock and lava layers of the Chisos, casting rich reds, vibrant pink and purple hues, and warm blues to form a palette Bob Ross might use to make happy little mountains. Lump in the diversity in flora and fauna—60 kinds of cacti, 450 species of birds,

mountain lions, black bears, gray foxes, and innumerable insects—and this isolated crook of Texas quickly
becomes a naturalist's dream. It is, as the National Park
Service puts it, a "magical place."

It's also huge: the park comprises 801,163 acres. The
vastness allows for 200-plus miles of hiking trails in the
park, and it's difficult to know where to start your journey.
For new and old visitors alike, the Window Trail is to Big
Bend as "Blue Eyes Crying in the Rain" is to Willie Nelson: an old and trusty standard that always pleases. The
descent down from the Chisos Mountain Lodge to the
"Window,"—a twenty-foot, v-shaped opening between
the rock formed by thousands of years of water erosion
from the Chisos Basin runoff—is truly awe-inspiring, a
picturesque frame of the western desert.

Beginner
If a multi-mile hike is too strenuous for you, opt for
the Window View Trail, a short .3-mile (wheelchair-
accessible) path from the Chisos Mountain Lodge parking lot. From here, you can get a wide shot of what you'll
see through the Window. Or, if you ask for the second
floor of Casa A at the lodge, you'll only have to walk out
to your balcony to enjoy the vistas.

Intermediate
If you have the time (around two hours) and the energy
(it's a 5.6-mile roundtrip hike from the Basin trailhead
near the lodge), slather on the sunscreen, grab your water
(plenty of it!), and trek toward the Window. As you leave
the Basin, you'll enter what is called Oak Creek Canyon.
After heavier rains, the stream will be running and parts

of the trail will be slick. Mind your footing, and gingerly cross back and forth across the water until you approach the Window. Don't venture too close to the edge; the eroded rocks are slippery, and a fall would send you more than 200 feet over the cliffside. Take time to mentally imprint the beauty of the sprawling desert on your brain; plus, you'll need the break to recharge your calves before embarking on the uphill return hike.

Advanced

Shave a mile off of your hike, and start at the Chisos Basin Campground trailhead (4.4-mile roundtrip and only a 500-foot elevation on the return trip). For a heightened experience, plan the hike so you're at the Window for sunset, but if you're hiking after dark, don't forget flashlights or headlamps. To see the Window from a different perspective, take the side trip to the Oak Spring Trail. There are some steep switchbacks, but if you follow the trail down, you will be rewarded with (yet another) incredible view of the park.

★ ★ ★

FURTHER READING

Carmack, Liz. *Historic Hotels of Texas: A Traveler's Guide.* College Station: Texas A&M University Press, 2007.

Pohlen, Jerome. *Oddball Texas: A Guide to Some Really Strange Places.* Chicago: Chicago Review Press, Incorporated, 2006.

Reavis, Dick. *Texas.* New York: Fodor's Compass American Guides, 1995.

Tarpley, Fred. *1001 Texas Place Names.* Austin: University of Texas Press, 1980.

Acknowledgments

I am compelled to personally thank the people who have made this book possible.

Beau, you've made me a better Texan. Thank you for loving me, for pushing me, for enduring my alternate states of giddiness and grumpiness during the writing process. For buying me dipped cones and doing extra chores and just leaving me alone when I needed it. I couldn't do this—life, that is—without you.

Mom, you've made me a better person. You are my biggest champion and most stalwart supporter, and without your unconditional love, I would not be where I am today. Thank you for wearing out the library card checking out books for me. For showing me how to work hard and teaching me to never settle for less. You're my inspiration.

Dad, you taught me the value of letters and language, and I can only hope to one day be as gifted a wordsmith as you. Thank you for all the trips to Bookstop and for letting us read whatever we wanted.

Philip, seeing my big brother gobble up books and furiously write late into the night inspired me to do the same, and to this day, you sharpen my wit with every conversation.

Abi Daniel, you are so damn talented, and I'm honored you agreed to partner with me on this project. I treasure our friendship and look forward to sharing endless glasses of bourbon and never-ending bowls of mussels.

Casey Kittrell, I'm not the first—nor will I be the last—to thank you for your endless patience and good nature. The publishing industry needs more humans like you.

My *Texas Monthly* family, how did I get so lucky to be counted among your ranks? I love you all, and I am especially grateful to Kate Rodemann and Brian D. Sweany, my acting editors on "The Manual," and Stacy Hollister, who made sure the page always made it to the printer. Special thanks also to the copy editors and fact checkers who made sure I didn't make too big a fool of myself (is that accurate? And did I spell all of that write?).

To the Kloses, who welcomed me into their family with unparalleled Texas hospitality. Y'all're the real deal. To Grandma and Grandpa Therwhanger, who taught Beau and me everything they know about 42—except how to beat them.

To my friends, who have been supportive of me, even though I've been AWOL for months. I'm back, y'all!

And a very special thanks to everyone who spoke to me throughout the reporting process. This book relies on the expertise and knowledge of these bona fide Texans. Without them this guide would bear no authenticity.